HALLOWEEN TRIVIA

HALLOWEEN TRIVIA

GHOSTS, GHOULS, SKELETONS, VAMPIRES, WITCHES, GRAVEYARDS, SPIDERS, ZOMBIES, HAUNTED HOUSES

Tonya Lambert

BLUE
BIKE
BOOKS

The Publisher: Blue Bike Books

Website: www.bluebikebooks.com

Library and Archives Canada Cataloguing in Publication

Lambert, Tonya Marie
    Halloween trivia : Ghosts, ghouls, skeletons, vampires, witches, graveyards, spiders, zombies, haunted houses / Tonya M. Lambert.

ISBN 978-1-926700-18-2

    1. Halloween—Miscellanea. 2. Halloween—History. I. Title.

GT4965.L35 2010   394.2646   C2010-901852-4

Project Director: Nicholle Carrière
Project Editor: Kathy van Denderen
Front Cover Image: © 2010 iStockphoto LP | 3Djml/Jean-Marc labal
Back Cover Image: Photos.com
Illustrations: Peter Tyler, Roger Garcia, Patrick Hénaff, Djordje Todorovic

We acknowledge the support of the Alberta Foundation for the Arts for our publishing program.

We acknowledge the financial support of the Government of Canada through the Book Publishing Industry Development Program (BPIDP) for our publishing activities.

PC: 1

DEDICATION

To my daughters,
Becky, Mary and Amy,
who enjoy Halloween so much.

Thank you for your supportive
patience, understanding and love.

CONTENTS

INTRODUCTION. 9

HALLOWEEN: THE CREATION OF A HOLIDAY
Samhain: A Gateway in Time. 12
Traversing the Bounds between Worlds 14
Ancient Celtic Gods Connected to Samhain 16
Modern Pagans and Samhain 20

HONORING THE DEAD
All Saints' Day 22
All Souls' Day. 24
All Souls' Day Around the World 30

MUMMIES
A Multitude of Mummies. 39

GRAVEYARDS AND TOMBSTONES
Tombstone Trivia 47
Coffins and Corpses. 53

SKELETONS
The Grim Reaper 60
Ghostly Skeletons 62

HALLOWEEN IN BETWEEN
The Evolution of Halloween. 66
Halloween: A Festival of Love? 71

WICKED WITCHES
The Time of the Witch Trials 75
Infamous Witch Hunters 83

CREEPY CREATURES
Black Cats. 93
Rats 100
Beware of Bats 101
Owls 105
Scary Spiders 108

SUPERNATURAL MONSTERS
Werewolves on the Prowl 114
Vicious Vampires 122
Zombies. 135
Freaky Frankenstein. 138

GHOULS, GHOSTS AND FAIRIES
Ghouls 140
Ghosts, Spirits and Specters 142
Fairies 153

CURIOUS CUSTOMS

You're the Apple of My Eye! 159

Halloween Divinations 165

Pumpkins and Punkies 175

Halloween Foods 179

HALLOWEEN TRADITIONS

Trick-or-Trivia! 182

Mischief Night 186

Halloween Costumes 190

Scary Haunts 194

Haunted Places 196

HALLOWEEN FESTIVITIES

Fairs and Festivals 203

Weddings 210

No More Halloween?! 213

The Spread of Halloween 217

INTRODUCTION

Halloween is my favorite holiday. I begin preparing for it at least one month in advance, choosing a costume and decorating the house and yard. I like this day so much for many reasons but mainly because it is unique in that it is devoted to fun. Halloween is a day when you can be whoever or whatever you want—a day for living fantasies and confronting fears. It is a time to joke and laugh, to socialize, indulge and celebrate life.

Halloween is largely a North American holiday, though it is making inroads into Europe and other regions of the world. Halloween is the fastest-growing holiday celebration, and only Christmas is more stimulating for the North American economy.

Nonetheless, although Halloween is widely enjoyed and celebrated, not everyone approves of it. Some church leaders espouse the erroneous belief that Halloween is a celebration of evil, a time of worshipping the Devil. However, symbols of death and scary images do not mean that people are promoting evil. It is simply a way of accepting that death is a part of life and learning to come to terms with that concept. Avoiding the discussion of death until it actually happens only makes it more difficult to deal with. As for scary images, the world is full of scary people and events.

For the early Celts, Halloween was a religious celebration, a time when the dead roamed the earth. For the

Victorians, the day was celebrated as a matchmaking event. For modern-day Wiccans, it is a time to honor the ancestors, to celebrate the end of one year and the beginning of the next.

The significant presence of scary figures on Halloween plays an important role in maintaining the present structure of society, including the desire for good to triumph over evil. Throughout history, people of all cultures have embraced periods of social inversion when the weak become powerful, the well behaved are able to act out and so on. These regularly occurring events are much-needed outlets for the tensions that grow within any rigid structure. By dressing as anti-authority figures and behaving in a riotous manner, people can release the pressure that builds within, during the day-to-day routine of tight schedules and social hierarchies. In short, festivals such as Halloween serve as safety valves for our society.

Today, such socially approved opportunities for fun-filled tension release are rare. In much of North America, Halloween is the only such holiday. Without structured and approved outlets for stress and frustration, people resort to other socially destructive avenues of release. The Puritans of England and New England tried to ban all holidays and celebrations, including Christmas, but were unable to do so. People need to have time for fun and celebration and merry-making. Individuals, as well as rigid social structures, require periods of release and inversion to function properly. You only have to see the smiles on children's faces and listen to the laughter of adults to understand how much they enjoy Halloween.

I hope this book will help to educate people, to show the roots of Halloween and the variety of ways it has been and is celebrated, depending on the purpose it serves in the people's lives. Fifty years ago, Halloween started as a holiday for children, but today it is an evening of merry-making for young and old alike.

Hopefully, this book will help to dispel some of the mistaken ideas surrounding this fun-filled holiday, as well as provide you with some interesting trivia about Halloween.

SAMHAIN: A GATEWAY IN TIME

Tying Up Loose Ends at the Year's End

Samhain was a festival of the ancient Celts since as far back as the fifth century BCE and was celebrated during the full moon at the end of October. Samhain was the most important festival of the Celtic year. It was when tribal assemblies were held, laws were made, contracts were negotiated and debts were paid. Samhain was a truce time with no fighting allowed. On this eve, the ancient Celts put out their hearth fires. Then, they met on hilltops with their Druid priests, who used oak branches to kindle a big bonfire. Later, the head of each household took embers from this fire back home to light new hearth fires, symbolizing the start of a new year.

Spirits at Samhain

The tradition of lighting bonfires at Samhain was to scare away evil spirits. The ancient Celts burned the bodies of dead animals to honor their gods, and it is from this practice that the term "bonfire" (for "bone fire") developed. Afterwards, the bones of the animals were used for divination.

To the Celts, Samhain was a gateway between years and seasons. It was the death of summer and the beginning of a new cycle of seasons. The night of Samhain was outside the cyclical bounds of time. On this night, chaos reigned—the past, present and future were all one and the same. The dead were able to return to the world of the living: some to visit loved ones, others to seek revenge and yet others to give the living a glimpse into the future. Some people dressed up in masks and costumes hoping to lure the evil spirits away from the settlements.

A Harvest Festival

Samhain was also believed to be the time of the annual mating of the fruit god Dagda with the river and war goddess Morrigan, resulting in offspring (the crops) nine months later—in July. It was also a harvest festival. Cattle were brought down from summer meadows in the mountains, and pigs were butchered. Drinking ale was another part of the Celtic celebration of Samhain. This may have been the sole time of year for drinking alcoholic beverages as there is ample archaeological evidence of brewing vats but not of storage containers.

Halloween III

Halloween III: Season of the Witch (1982) is a unique horror movie in that it explores the historical aspects of Halloween rather than simply presenting another scary film about current customs. In the movie, Irishman Conal Cochran (played by Daniel O'Herlihy) runs a toy factory that specializes in Halloween products. Inspired by tales of ancient sacrifices of children at Samhain, Cochran puts chips from Stonehenge's bluestone inside masks programmed to explode at 9:00 PM on October 31.

DID YOU  KNOW?

The first *Halloween* movie was filmed in only 21 days in 1978.

TRAVERSING THE BOUNDS BETWEEN WORLDS

The Lifting of the Veil

The ancient Celts believed that each year at Samhain, the veil between the world of the dead and the supernatural and the world of the living lifted, allowing the inhabitants of each world to travel freely to the other. This was because Samhain, as the end of one year and the beginning of another, was a brief period outside the realm of time during which the natural rules of the world did not apply.

Numerous legends of the ancient Celts speak to this belief that Samhain was a time when the boundaries between the worlds was thinnest. The legend of Nera is one such tale. The story of Finn and the goblin is another. In Ireland, a big cave still bears the name "Hell Gate of Ireland," which is thought to open on Halloween to let out the spirits of the dead.

The Legend of Nera

At the court of Queen Mebd and King Ailill of Connacht, two captives were hanged on the day before Samhain. The next day, the king offered a prize—his gold-hilted sword—to anyone who would tie a band of willow twigs around the foot of one of the bodies, as doing this was believed to keep the body's spirit at rest. Many brave men tried but all failed because of their fears of the spirits roaming about on Samhain. Nera finally succeeded with help from the dead man himself. In return for his assistance, the dead man asked Nera for a drink, but it took the pair some time before they found a place willing to serve the dead man. Upon their return, they found the royal fortress in flames and all the people killed.

Nera himself was captured by the spirits of the Otherworld that night. They placed him in the custody of a female spirit and ordered him to bring the Spirit King a bundle of firewood every day. Soon, Nera and the spirit woman fell in love and secretly married. She revealed to her husband that the destruction of Mebd and Ailill's fortress had not yet occurred but it would if the fairy mound at Cruachan cave was not destroyed before two Samhains had passed. Nera left the Otherworld and went to warn the court of Connacht. While he was gone, the spirit woman delivered the daily bundle of firewood to the Spirit King. She also bore Nera a son. When the other men left to destroy the fairy mound, Nera chose to return to the Otherworld to be with his family.

Legend of Finn and the Goblin

The ancient Celtic legend of Finn and the goblin tells of the destruction of Tara (north of present-day Dublin) by evil fairies each Samhain. Every year at Samhain, the Celts who gathered at the royal seat of Tara were lulled into a deep sleep by the harp music of a goblin named Aillen. And each year while they slept, Aillen would set fire to the royal fortress, destroying it and everything within it. One year, however, the warrior Finn managed to remain awake by poking himself in the forehead with his spear, causing himself great pain. He thwarted the mischievous plans of Aillen, who never returned to Tara again.

ANCIENT CELTIC GODS CONNECTED TO SAMHAIN

Cailleach Bheur

The Celtic goddess of winter, Cailleach Bheur, is said to be reborn every year on October 31. She reigns until April 30, the eve of Beltane.

Scottish farmers used to leave the last sheaf of grain in the field after harvest and would not cut it before Halloween. However, on that day, it was imperative that the sheaf be cut down before nightfall or else it would turn into a wicked witch. This sheaf was known as the Cailleach, or last sheaf, named after the ancient Celtic goddess of the same name. Clothes were wrapped around the sheaf to form a dress and apron, the pockets of which were filled with bread and cheese. The farmer's wife sometimes danced around with the Cailleach on her back. At the farmhouse, the Cailleach was given a place of honor, where it stood until the feast of Beltane six months later, on May 1. Into the 20th century, Scottish farmers were still leaving a stalk of grain standing in their fields after harvest to appease the sometimes-cruel Cailleach Bheur.

It was customary in southwest Scotland and in the Irish province of Ulster (now Northern Ireland and largely colonized by the Scots) to name the man who cut the last sheaf of grain the guest of honor at the Halloween celebrations. The Cailleach was placed over the door to the house. In some areas, the first woman to enter could be kissed by all the reapers. In other areas, she was believed to be the next woman to marry while the man who had cut the sheaf was to be the next man to wed.

The Dagda and the Morrigan

The Dagda was a wiseman of the invading group, the Tuatha De. In a quest to defeat the Fomorian inhabitants of the island, the Dagda met with the Morrigan, a warrior goddess, at Samhain every year for seven years in order to learn from her the plans of the Fomorians. The final battle between the Fomorians and the Tuatha De began on the eve of Samhain and continued for several days, with the Tuatha De finally forcing the Fomorians to retreat under the sea.

The Dagda became a god. Every year thereafter, the Dagda and the Morrigan would meet at Samhain and consummate their union, thereby ensuring fertility throughout the land in the coming year.

Nicnevin

Nicnevin, an ancient Scottish deity, is known as the Crone of Samhain. Little is known today about this deity, who is mentioned in several 16th-century Scottish works, including the 1508 poem "Flyting" by Dunbar and the 1590 treatise *Complaynt of Scotland* by Lindsay.

Shoney

On the island of Lewis in Scotland, an annual libation to Shoney, an ancient god of the sea, was performed up until the time of the Restoration in 1660.

At nightfall on Halloween, the islanders marched down to the seashore after having gathered at the Chapel of St. Malvey to pray and say the Paternoster ("Our Father") together. A member of the community would then wade into the water carrying a cup of ale. Before pouring it into the sea, he would beseech Shoney to provide the islanders with good fishing in the coming year. He would also ask that plenty of seaweed be cast up on the shore so the inhabitants could use it to fertilize their fields. Following this offering, the islanders returned to the chapel for a period of silent prayer. Afterward, the more lively festivities of the holiday were enjoyed by all.

Ireland and Muck Olla

Beginning in the medieval period, people in Ireland went begging in groups from door to door in October. The groups would request offerings in the name of Muck Olla. (It is no longer known who Muck Olla was—not even if he was a deity or not.) In some areas, this begging for treats took place up to a month before Halloween. The leader of the group, known as the Lair Bhan, or White Mare, dressed in white and wore a mask of a horse's head (likely a horse's skull in the early days of the practice).

In order to ensure continued good luck, farmers and their wives gave gifts of food to the groups for Muck Olla. At every farmhouse, the Lair Bhan recited a string of verses that accorded the farmer's good fortunes to Muck Olla:

> *Halloween is coming on and the goose is getting fat.*
> *Will you put a penny in the old lad's hat?*
> *If you haven't got a penny, a ha'penny will do.*
> *If you haven't got a ha'penny, a farthing will do.*
> *If you haven't got a farthing, then a piece of bread will do.*
> *If you haven't got a piece of bread,*
> *God bless you, and your old lad, too.*

This tradition of begging in groups was still being followed in some places in Ireland at the beginning of the 20th century.

The custom of going from farm to farm with a horse's head begging for food was also performed by men in Wales. The horse's skull was painted and set on a pole. The jaws were wired in such a way that the man carrying the skull could make them snap. The skull and the man carrying it were known as the Mari Lwyd or Gray Mare. If two groups of men encountered each other, they fought until one group had captured the horse's head of the other group.

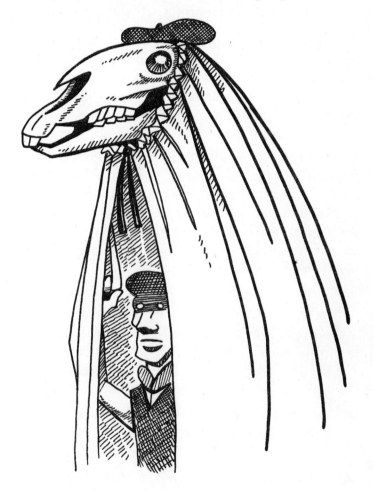

MODERN PAGANS AND SAMHAIN

Samhain, Wiccans and Neopagans

For pagans, Halloween (or Samhain or Shadowfest or Festival of the Dead) is the most sacred of the year's eight "sabbats." It is a time to honor the dead, to welcome in a new year, to celebrate the harvest, and to mourn the passing of the Horned God (who has no connection whatsoever to the evil Satan of Christianity and Judaism).

Most modern pagans adorn their homes and altars with images of skeletons and ghosts on All Hallows' Eve. This is a means of recognizing their belief in reincarnation, welcoming the spirits of departed loved ones and honoring the many gods and goddesses of the Underworld. Because black is the preferred color of the latter, many pagans wear black outfits on this evening as a show of respect.

- Samhain is one of the eight annual sabbats celebrated by Wiccans. The other seven are Yule (on the winter solstice), Imbolc (February 2), Ostara (on the vernal equinox), Beltane (May 1), Midsummer (on the summer solstice), Lugnasadh (August 1) and Mabon (on the autumnal equinox).

- On October 31, 1967, the New Reformed Orthodox Order of the Golden Dawn, a Wiccan organization, was formed in San Francisco.

- The first public pagan gathering in North America was authorized for New York City on October 31, 1970, and was held in Central Park. Well over 1000 people attended. It was organized by the Witches International Craft Association (WICA).

- Since 1972, the Church and School of Wicca has held an annual Samhain Seminar, which usually takes place in Durham, North Carolina.

- On October 31, 1979, Starhawk's book *The Spiral Dance* was released. It introduced a form of Dianic witchcraft that would later evolve into the empowering feminist witchcraft known as Reclaiming Wicca.

- On October 31, 1979, Margot Adler's book, *Drawing Down the Moon*, was published, a key work in the Neopagan and Wiccan movements. It explained these spiritual and religious practices as well as presented some of their practitioners.

- The Covenant of the Goddess, the largest Wiccan federation, was formed on Halloween 1975.

- In Bellaire, Texas, the Samhain Festival sponsored by the Council of the Magical Arts is held annually on the weekend closest to November 1.

- More than 2000 people participate in the Reclaiming Coven's Samhain Spiral Dance in San Francisco each year.

DID YOU KNOW?

Ireland is the only country in the world where Halloween is a national holiday. Schools in Ireland close for the celebration.

ALL SAINTS' DAY

Calling All Saints

November 1 is All Saints' or All Hallows' ("Holy Ones")
Day. It was instituted by the Catholic Church in 731 and
was originally celebrated on May 13, a date chosen because
it was the final day of the old pagan Roman festival known
as Lemuria, during which the spirits of the restless dead were
placated. In 835, the date was switched to November 1 to
coincide with celebrations honoring the dead still practiced
in Celtic countries on October 31.

Bell-ringing was a prominent part of medieval rituals on All
Saints. This practice was thought to comfort the many souls
caught in Purgatory. This custom ceased in those areas of
Europe that adopted Protestantism. In those areas that
remained Catholic, the bells are still rung today.

Medieval churches displayed the relics of saints on All Saints'
Day. Parish churches did not have such relics, so a parishioner or
two would dress up as the local patron saint(s) and lead a proces-
sion in which the other parishioners dressed as angels or demons.
It is thought the modern custom of dressing up in costumes for
Halloween may have developed from this earlier practice.

Feasting the Saints

Bread or cakes were traditionally distributed to the poor on
All Saints' Day in many countries.

- In Protestant England, some people in Lancashire and
  Hertfordshire still distributed bread to the poor on All
  Saints' Day in 1674. The poor would thank the saints,
  saying, "God have your soul, bones and all."

- In New Mexico, food is given to the parish priest on
  All Saints' Day.

🔔 In Trinidad, food prepared on All Saints' Day is not salted. People there also believe that the wax from the candles burned on this day has special curative abilities. Thus, the wax is kept and stored for use against colds and rheumatism.

🔔 Today, All Saints' Day is a public holiday in many Roman Catholic countries. In France, it is called *La Touissant*. In Bolivia, it is known as the day of "our living with the dead." It is a time for feasting with an extra place set for the dead. There are people called *Mihuqs*, who eat for the dead. In Spain, cakes and nuts are placed on graves the night before All Saints' Day to bribe restless spirits to not disturb the following day's solemn remembrances.

In the U.S., one All Saints' Day tradition is to remain silent throughout the evening meal. This is supposed to encourage the spirits to come to the meal. Africans brought this custom to the Americas.

DID YOU KNOW?

The Santiago Atitlan Indians of Guatemala celebrate All Saints' Day by flying kites. They believe that by doing so they will have a more direct line of communication with their departed ancestors in heaven.

ALL SOULS' DAY

A Feast Day for All Christian Souls

In the calendar of the Roman Catholic Church, November 2 is the Feast Day for All Souls, also known as "All Souls' Day." It is also informally known as "black vespers" because the church is decorated in black, the color of death. All Souls is a day for remembering and praying for the souls of the dead. The celebration dates back to at least the eighth century and possibly earlier. For many people, especially in times past, All Hallows' Eve or Halloween (October 31), All Saints' Day (November 1) and All Souls' Day (November 2) were inextricably linked in a three-day commemoration of the dead.

Legend states that All Souls' Day had its beginnings at the monastery of Cluny in France. Odilo, abbot of Cluny from 994 till his death in about 1048, is said to have received a visit from a pilgrim returning from the Holy Land. The pilgrim reported to the abbot that on his trip, he had been shipwrecked on an island, where he met a hermit. The hermit told him of a huge flaming gorge from which emanated the dreadful groans of the tormented souls trapped in Purgatory. Abbot Odilo is supposed to have initiated All Souls' Day to pray for these poor souls.

An earlier reference to a celebration for the souls of all the dead on the day following All Saints' Day is found in Amalarius' *De Ordine antiphonarii*. Amalarius lived in the eighth century. Some historians have speculated that this feast day for all Christian souls was another example of the Christian religion incorporating the traditions of the existing pagan religions whenever it was unable to eradicate them. Regardless, it appears that Abbot Odilo was not the originator of All Souls' Day. However, he was a leading proponent of the tradition and was instrumental in its spread throughout western Europe. Odilo wrote that justification for such a Feast Day was to be found in the Bible, in 2 Maccabees 12:46: "Therefore he made atonement for the dead, so that they might be set free from their sin." Despite the famous abbot's arguments, the date was not officially established by the papal authorities until the 14th century.

All Hallows' Eve was wiped from the church calendar in England during the Reformation because of its pagan associations. In 1928, the Church of England restored it to the calendar, mistakenly believing that it had finally lost its pagan associations.

From Samhain to All Souls in Brittany

The province of Brittany in northwestern France sticks far out into the Atlantic Ocean. This area was once part of the vast territories controlled by the Celtic peoples of ancient Europe. Standing on the shoreline, a person is closer to those other areas where the echoes of the Celtic past can still be heard—Cornwall, Wales and Ireland—than any other place on the Continent. Watching the waves roll toward the shore on All Souls' Day, one is reminded of the Breton proverb that states a corpse resides in the hollow of every wave. Indeed, in Brittany, fishermen did not go to sea between All Hallows' Eve (October 31) and All Souls' Day (November 2) lest they catch human bones in their nets.

Like their Celtic forebears, the people of Brittany still honor the dead at this time of the year by attending church services to pay homage to the saints on November 1, All Saints' Day. In the evening, families go to the cemetery to clean up the graves of deceased loved ones. Cider and pancakes are set out for the souls to enjoy when they visit the following day. While the adults tidy the gravesites, the youngsters play tricks, trying to frighten the people present. Sometimes the children will put a bone in a tin pail or can and rattle it while hiding out of sight behind a tombstone. After the graves are put in order, the people make their way to the charnel house where the bones of those long dead are housed. Here, families are able to touch the bones of their ancestors and reconnect with the past. On the days of All Saints and All Souls, the dead are very much alive in Brittany.

In the mid-19th century, the Breton people would file past the final resting places of their dead on November 2, reciting the names of the deceased as they passed. No one there does any digging on this day so as not to accidentally disturb anyone's remains. (In the event that this does happen, grain—preferably wheat—is planted on the spot so the souls of the saints will come to bless the location.)

It is considered sinful to not give the dead their due respect on All Souls' Day, and an old Breton folktale about a man named Yann Postick warns of the fate that will befall any person who fails to do so. In the story, Postick spends the eve of All Souls' Day drinking in a tavern rather than honoring the memories of departed family members at their graves. On his way home from the pub, he takes a wrong turn at a crossroads and comes upon a hearse drawn by black horses. The coachman says to him, "I seek Yann Postick," and Yann is quickly seized by three female spirits who command him to wash a death shroud. As he struggles with the three spirits, the shroud becomes wound tighter and tighter around him. The women chant, "Forever we must wash our linens, in the rain, the snow and the wind. Cursed be he who forgets to pray for his dead." Finally, three faces appear to Yann—his dead mother, wife and sister. The next day, Yann is found dead. At his funeral, the candles refuse to stay lit, which is a sign of evil. Consequently, Yann is buried in unconsecrated ground.

DID YOU KNOW?

A proverb from Brittany states that there are more souls in each house on All Souls' Day than there are grains of sand on the shores of the sea.

All Souls' Day in England

The following 17th-century "souling" song from Shropshire, England, shows that All Souls' Day was celebrated in that country long after the Protestant Reformation of the previous century:

> *A Soule-cake, a Soule-cake,*
> *Have mercy on all Christian soules for a soule-cake.*

Sometime during the Middle Ages, poor people started going door to door begging for money or for something to eat on All Souls' Day. Perhaps they felt that the prevailing mood of remembering the dear departed would also make people more aware of the suffering of their fellows, as this Somerset souling song suggests:

> *My clothes are very ragged*
> *My shoes are very thin*
> *I've got a little pocket*
> *To put three halfpence in*
> *And I'll never come a-souling*
> *Till another year.*

People who went door to door in this manner were known as "soulers" because of their promises to pray for the dead in exchange for food or money. The most common dole was buns with currants known as "soul cakes" (or "dirge loaves" in Scotland). Even in areas where people ceased to go souling following the Reformation, soul cakes were still made and kept for visitors on that day.

Souling seems to have survived in some areas of England and Wales (as well as in Austria) following the Reformation, more as a form of annual charity to the poor at the beginning of the difficult winter months. This appears to be the case in Cheshire, where this souling song was sung:

> *Cold winter it is coming on, dark, dirty, wet and cold,*
> *To try your good nature, this night we do make bold.*

In some areas of England, such as Shropshire and Cheshire, children still go out souling. They ride about on hobby horses, a remnant of an old belief that the souls of the dead were borne away on the backs of horses. Indeed, in one area of Wales, the custom of souling was referred to as "collecting the food of the messenger of the dead."

Peter stands at yonder gate
Waiting for a Soul Cake.

–Staffordshire souling song

Mumming

Another English holiday custom was the performance of "mumming" plays. These plays were performed at Christmas or on All Souls' Day, with the latter sometimes being referred to as "souling plays." After World War II, only three places still put on these plays: Great Budworth, Comberbach and Antrobus. Only the latter at Antrobus in Cheshire is still performed. The play is presented around the area for two weeks following Halloween, when it is always done in Antrobus.

All mumming plays feature a combat between two heroes. One is injured and a doctor is sent for. Much haggling over the doctor's fees ensues, but an agreement is finally reached, and the hero is healed.

The money raised by the play is donated to charity to purchase food for the poor. Thus, the original purpose of the play, to raise money for the poor, still continues. Indeed, during the performance, a hobby horse chastises tight-fisted neighbors to be generous to the poor around them. Following the play, the actors, known as "soulers" or "soulcakers," accept donations from audience members.

Immigrants from the British Isles brought the tradition of mumming plays to Canada, the U.S. and the island of St. Kitts, though the custom did not survive long in the new locales.

ALL SOULS' DAY AROUND THE WORLD

All Souls' Day Customs in Poland

- Doors and windows are left open to welcome the visiting spirits of deceased family members.

- The names of deceased loved ones are written on sheets of white paper with black borders, and these are taken to the parish priest so that prayers will be offered up for these souls throughout the month of November.

- Souls in Purgatory are believed to gather in churches at midnight on All Souls' Day to pray for their release.

- Children pray aloud in the woods so that the souls of the deceased will hear them and be comforted.

German Celebrations of All Souls' Day

- On All Souls' Day in Germany, church bells are rung at noon, releasing souls from Purgatory until noon the next day.

- Bowls of butter and fat are left out to heal the wounds of the dead, as well as cold milk to cool their souls.

- Knives are hidden so the spirits are not harmed accidentally.

- It was believed that if you made a wish while walking around a church three times on All Souls' Day, it would come true.

- In Catholic areas of Germany, families left a single candle (blessed on Candlemas Day) lit, said the rosary and prayed on the evening of All Souls' Day.

All Souls' Day in South America

Throughout Latin America, All Souls' Day is a public holiday.

In Ecuador, El Salvador and Uruguay, the day is marked by a special mass followed by a procession to the local cemetery.

In Peru, people who resemble deceased loved ones are invited to share the food of the family gathered at the cemetery on the night of All Souls' Day. The food eaten by the look-alike is believed to feed the departed family member.

In Columbia, a bell ringer and a cross bearer lead groups of children in a march. They go from house to house singing, "Angels are we, from heaven we come, asking alms, for ourselves." People toss fruit to the children. In the past, the fruit was taken to the church, cooked and eaten (with the souls in Purgatory, it was thought), but now, the fruit is taken home and shared with family members and neighbors.

All Souls' Day in Italy

Italy, the heart of Roman Catholicism, has long embraced the celebration of All Souls' Day. Remembrance rituals for the dead in Italy pre-date the Church by many centuries, however.

The Romans held a festival called Feralia honoring the dead every year at the end of October.

During the Middle Ages, the poor in Italy were given fava bean soup on All Souls' Day. For Italians, beans have long been symbolic of death. Today, Italians eat bean-shaped bread known as "Beans of the Dead" on November 2.

☠ In Rome, All Souls is a popular day for engagements, with the man having the ring delivered to his girlfriend in an oval container filled with bean-shaped cakes made of ground almonds, sugar, eggs, butter and flour.

☠ In 14th-century Salerno, people left out food in their homes for the spirits, leaving the door open for them to enter. If the food remained untouched come nightfall, it was a sign of future bad luck. Of course, it was actually beggars and thieves who took the food. The Church banned the practice in the 15th century because of its strong pagan associations.

☠ In northern Italy, people left their beds empty on the night before All Souls so that wandering spirits would have a place to rest. In Corsica, people still leave jugs of water out for the dead to quench their thirst.

☠ On the eve of All Souls' Day, the people of Naples used to dress up the exposed skeletons of dead relatives. On All Souls' Day, these well-dressed skeletons would receive their guests. Relatives would write their names on the tombs of their ancestors and even leave calling cards. Skulls, bones and other symbols of death decorate the cakes and candies sold in Sicily and Perugia on this day.

☠ In modern Italy, All Souls' Day begins with a requiem mass at dawn, followed by a visit to the cemetery to place flowers and candles on the graves. In Sicily, following the graveyard visit, children

PRESENTS IN SHOES PLEASE

leave their shoes outside the door of their homes to be filled with gifts. The children are told that the toys and treats that they receive are gifts from their ancestors.

☠ A traditional Sicilian All Souls' Day treat is *martorana*, a marzipan candy made in the shape of various fruit. The candy was originally made by a Benedictine order of nuns in Palermo.

☠ In many areas of Italy, a candle is lit or a lamp left on during the night to welcome the spirits of the deceased. (This custom is also carried out in Belgium and the Philippines.)

The Pueblo Natives

👻 The Cochiti Pueblo Natives of New Mexico call All Souls' Day "Their Grandfathers Arrive from the Dead Feast." The purpose is to both honor the dead and to assure them that their descendents are prospering. In order to prove the latter, the family's material possessions are put on display in the house. The family fasts. The men and boys spend the night in a ceremonial chamber, where they sing songs and cut up food for the dead.

👻 The Taos Pueblo Natives take food to the graves at night. Candles are lit in churches and houses in the belief that the dead will burn the fingertips of those who fail to light their way. Church bells are rung throughout the night.

👻 At about the same time as All Souls' Day, the Zuni Pueblo Natives celebrate Grandmothers' Day by offering food to the dead. Also, men and boys go from house to house singing and receiving food.

Soul Cakes

The practice of giving cakes to feed the souls of the dead has a long and widespread history. In countries that practice the Roman Catholic faith, an old tradition holds that for every soul cake eaten, a soul will be released from Purgatory. In Britain, different regions prepare different types of soul cakes:

- In Yorkshire, soul cakes were dark fruitcakes.

- In Northamptonshire, soul cakes were small buns covered in caraway seeds.

- In Scotland, soul cakes were round, flat buns made of oat flour.

- In Chichester, cakes with white icing were eaten on All Saints' Day. The white icing was said to symbolize the saints.

- In northern England in the early 20th century, mothers still baked soul cakes for their children, each a different flavor. The day was known as Cake Day.

Feeding the Dead

Other countries also have traditions of feeding the departed:

- In ancient Egypt, families left cakes inside tombs for the *ka* of deceased relatives.

- The Ainu people of Japan make millet cakes for their dead. On the Japanese festival for the dead, called Bon, people leaves cakes for the returning souls beside their shrines for three days.

- Hindus leave honeyed rice balls out for the spirits of the dead.

- The Chinese prepare little cakes and other delicacies for their Festival for the Hungry Ghosts.

The Aztec Days of the Dead

The Days of the Dead (*Los Días de los Muertos*) celebrations in present-day Mexico are a combination of the rituals conducted by the Spanish colonists for All Saints' and All Souls' days with those traditions of the native Aztec inhabitants of the area.

Mictlin

The Aztec underworld was known as Mictlin. A soul's journey to Mictlin was long and fraught with peril. It took four years to accomplish, and it was not until then that the soul could rest peacefully.

Like Dante's Inferno, Mictlin was a multi-leveled place. In each of the nine levels dwelt souls united in their manner of death, such as war or childbirth. Only the ninth and final level was less unified in nature, simply accommodating all those souls who did not fit neatly into any of the other eight levels. It was the most crowded level in Mictlin. This lowest level was ruled over by the husband and wife deities, Miclantecuhtli and Mictecacihuatl.

Miclantecuhtli

Miclantecuhtli was the Aztec god of death and the night. Both he and his wife were depicted as ferocious skeletal beings with protruding teeth and organs hanging from their rib cages. Mictecacihuatl frequently accessorized with an equally gruesome necklace of human eyeballs. Yet, despite their fierce appearance, Miclantecuhtli was seen as a kind deity who released people from the burdens of this world to the pleasures of the next.

Celebrating the Dead

The Aztec celebrations of the dead were much longer than those held currently, lasting two months rather than three days. However, they were divided between those for children (Miccailhuitontli) and those for adults (Miccailhuitl) in the manner continued by their descendants, today.

The Aztecs would place rushes, reeds and sedge on their altars. At dawn, these altars would be decorated with images of the dead, gifts of food and incense in a ceremony called *calonoac*. Another custom involved decorating a tree with gifts. People competed to see who could climb up and reach the highest gift. The person who climbed the highest was said to have made it closest to the gods and the ancestors.

Mexico's Days of the Dead

The Natives of Mesoamerica used to have an annual festival honoring the dead. European missionaries combined these festivities with the Christian rituals surrounding Halloween, All Saints' and All Souls' days. Today, this celebration is known as *Los Días de los Muertos* (Days of the Dead).

November 1 is the day set aside to remember dead children, while November 2 is for remembering dead adults. At midnight on November 1, Mexican women and girls take flowers, food and candles to the cemetery to honor the dead, while the men and boys sing songs for the dead outside the cemetery gates. At dawn, everyone enjoys a meal together among the graves.

In some areas of Mexico, the Days of the Dead encompass more than the usual three days: October 27 is for the souls of people who died without a family, October 28 is for those who died a violent death, October 30 is for infants who died before being baptized, and October 31 is for baptized infants.

A National Holiday

In Mexico, Days of the Dead are a national holiday. Celebrations vary from region to region, with some emphasizing household altars, others public shrines, and some focus on the procession to the cemetery while still others give the most attention to the graves.

- In Janitzio, one custom that occurs on the evening of November 1 is that the youth of the town go about "stealing" fruit and vegetables from the houses and fields. These are then taken to the community center where a feast is prepared as part of that night's vigil. The next day, these same youths go from house to house asking for donations of food, which are then taken to the priest, who offers up special prayers for the dead.

- In Pancanda, the people keeping vigil face the east at dawn to witness the sunrise, which indicates the rebirth of life.

- In the P'urhepecha Plateau region of western Mexico, the dead were once buried with a brown dog. It was felt that because the dog could see in the dark, it would lead the deceased on their journey as well as on their return each November 1.

- In the Michoacan area of western Mexico, stars are thought to be the souls of the dead.

Marigolds: Follow the Yellow *Petal* Road

Mexicans have continued another Aztec practice, that of using marigolds (the flower of the dead) to lure the wandering souls of loved ones back home. Marigolds can be seen everywhere during Days of the Dead. They are planted in August so they will be in bloom by the end of October. In Santa Cruz, marigold petals are scattered from the graves of loved ones to their former homes to guide their way back. Often, decorative crosses and wreathes of marigolds are placed on the graves of loved ones.

Skulls and Skeletons

Skeletons are frequently seen in Mexico on the Days of the Dead. Children dress as ghosts, monsters and mummies and parade about town crying out for skulls (that is, candy skulls, treats, fruit or money). People even eat bread shaped like skulls ("Dead Men's Bread"). The Days of the Dead also includes picnics at the cemetery accompanied by items cherished by the departed or by skeletons dressed as or doing something the deceased enjoyed. Mexicans clear weeds from the graves and also scrub and sweep the crypts and tombstones.

Skeletons often feature as decorative elements on the satiric newspapers and *calaveras* printed across the country on Days of the Dead. Calaveras are satirical poems about popular public figures on All Saints' Day in Mexico; they mock the notion that these leaders are "saintly."

Strengthening Social Bonds Past and Present

Days of the Dead celebrations in Mexico strengthen community ties. People remember and honor dead friends and relatives by constructing altars in their home at this time of year. On the altar are photos and mementos of the dead along with items symbolizing the four elements: fire (candles), air/wind (tissue flowers or other items that will blow away in a breeze), earth (food—the dead eat by smelling it) and water. In some Mexican villages today, young engaged men whose fathers have died go to the grave to announce their engagement and gain their father's permission.

In Mexico, death is the time for mourning, but the Days of the Dead is a time for remembering—the former is sad, the latter happy. Mexicans, like the Aztecs before them, believe that the millions of monarch butterflies that arrive in the country at this time of year are the souls of the dead returning for their annual visit.

A MULTITUDE OF MUMMIES

Preserving the Bodies of the Dead

Since the discovery of Tutankhamen's tomb in Egypt's Valley of the Kings in 1922, mummies have been a popular part of Halloween decorations and costumes. A mummy costume is easy to make—a person simply wraps himself up in yards of bandages or cut-up sheets.

The ancient Egyptians mummified their dead so that the deceased person would have a body in the afterlife. Egyptians believed that each person had two spirits—the *ba* and the *ka*. Following the burial of the body, the person's ba would leave the tomb and maintain contact with loved ones, while the ka remained in the burial chamber. When the ba decided to return to its body and join with the ka to become the *akh*, it could only do so if it was able to identify its body. This is why it was so important to the Egyptians that people's bodies be well preserved.

Making a Mummy

The quality of mummification varied according to a person's ability to pay. Embalmers and priests (who recited special prayers) carried out the process. It took 70 days to mummify a body. First, the brain was removed bit by bit through the nose and discarded. Next, the liver, stomach, lungs and intestines were removed and placed in individual canopic jars so they could accompany the rest of the body on its voyage. Each jar was topped with the head of one of the four sons of the god Horus the Younger—human-headed Imsety held the liver, jackal-headed Duamutef the stomach, baboon-headed Hapy the lungs and hawk-headed Qebehsenuef the intestines. The heart, regarded as the seat of the intellect and emotions by the Egyptians, remained in the body and was covered with a protective scarab amulet.

After the internal organs were removed, natron, a blend of four different salts from the Nile, was used to dry out the corpse, a process that took 40 days. Next, the corpse was stuffed with sawdust, linen and resin until it had regained its original shape. Finally, the body was wrapped in linen cloth with various protective amulets hidden within. A shroud enveloped the form. Wealthier individuals had their bodies placed in one or more sarcophagi (stone coffins).

Tickle Your Funny Bone

Why was the mummy so tense?
He was all wound up!

Why don't mummies take vacations?
They are afraid to unwind.

What type of music do mummies like most?
Wrap music.

What type of underwear do mummies wear?
Fruit of the Tomb!

What happened when the boy mummy met the girl mummy?
It was love at first fright!

DID YOU  KNOW?

In 19th-century Europe, wealthy aristocrats purchased mummies and then invited guests over for an unwrapping!

Mummies as Medicine

The renowned 10th-century Persian physician Avicenna believed that ground mummy dust was a cure for a whole host of ailments, including diseases of the liver and spleen, rashes, paralysis and constipation. His writings are the earliest known reference to the medicinal use of mummies.

The medicinal use of ground mummies was popular in Europe between the 12th and 19th centuries. The French king Francis I reputedly ate rhubarb with mummy dust every day in the hopes of protecting himself against assassination. To further protect himself, he also carried a small packet of mummy dust with him at all times.

When the supply of ancient mummies ran low in the 15th century, some unscrupulous merchants in Egypt began to mummify the bodies of those recently deceased, including the corpses of those who had died from various diseases. This was discovered by Guy de la Fontaine, physician to the King of Navarre, on a trip to Egypt (*mizraim*, the term used by European apothecaries for mummy dust is ancient Hebraic for Egypt) to obtain more mummies. There, he visited the shop of the chief mummy merchant in the city of Alexandria to discover that the man had been making his own mummies from any bodies he was able to obtain by filling them with bitumen and leaving them out in the sun to dry.

This did not stop Europeans from using powdered mummies for all sorts of ailments. Indeed, the pharmaceutical company of E. Merck was still advertising this product for sale in the early 20th century!

Mummies as Paint

Besides ground-up mummies being used as a type of medicinal cure-all, the powder was also employed as the base for a pigment used by 17th- and 18th-century artists. The color was referred to as "mummy brown."

Wrapping Paper from Bandages

Not only were mummified bodies sold and used but so, too, were the bandages used to wrap them. Shortages of linen during the American Civil War (1861–65) resulted in the importation of mummy bandages for use in the manufacture of plain brown wrapping paper.

Mummies Throughout History

- The earliest mummies were made by the Chinchorro people of present-day northern Chile around 7000 years ago.

- In 1599, the Capuchin monks of Palermo discovered by accident that bodies placed in their airtight limestone crypt mummified. For the next three centuries, the citizens of Palermo formed a new underground city of mummies—all dressed in their Sunday best with the bodies arranged according age, gender and social status.

- Naples, situated at the base of Mt. Vesuvius, has soil rich in volcanic ash, an ideal mummification agent. For centuries, deceased Neapolitans have been buried without coffins for 1.5 to 2 years, at which point their mummified bodies are dug up and placed in familial burial vaults located above ground.

- The Dani people of Irian Jaya, Indonesia, used to smoke the bodies of important leaders to preserve them. This allowed the living to continue to access the wisdom of the deceased leader. Today, these mummies are tourist attractions with which a person can get a photo taken for a fee.

- In 1865, officials in Guanajuato, Mexico, went to remove from graves at Panteon Cemetery the remains of those whose families had ceased to pay the local annual burial tax. They discovered that the bodies had mummified because of the area's extremely arid conditions. The remains were still removed from their graves but were placed in a special mummy museum—Museo de los Momias. There are now more than 100 mummies on display, including those of tiny premature infants. Approximately 800,000 tourists visit the museum annually.

In Borneo, the recently deceased are placed in large earthenware jars. These jars are regularly emptied of bodily fluids that have drained from the corpse. When only the dry mummified remains are left, they are moved to another jar. The original jar is then cleaned and used for cooking. Yuck!

A company called Summum, in Salt Lake City, Utah, offers mummification services. It was founded in the 1970s by Claude Nowell. The body is preserved by being soaked in a secret formula. The brain is removed and mummified separately before being replaced. The body is then oiled and wrapped in layers of polyure- thane and linen. Resin is then used to cover it. Finally, the body is placed in an airtight, Egyptian-style coffin.

Animal Mummies

More animals than humans were mummified in ancient Egypt.

Egyptian mythology told of how the creator god Ptah inhabited the body of a bull in order to live on earth. The bull in which Ptah resided was known as the Apis bull. This bull was worshipped at Memphis. When an Apis bull died, it was mummified and placed in a crypt called the Serapeum at Saqqara. A new Apis bull was then sought out. It could be identified by special markings on its body.

Many ancient Egyptian deities were comprised of both human and animal body parts. Animals were mummified so they could be presented as offerings to the deity who bore their features. Thus, cat mummies were presented to the goddess Bastet at Bubastis. Dogs were given to the deities Anubis, god of mummification, and Wepwawet, the opener god. Thoth, the god of wisdom, was offered mummies of the ibis bird, while the goddess Hatmehit received fish. The god Sobek was the recipient of many mummified crocodile offerings at Shedyet and Kom Ombo.

Cat mummies were so numerous in Egypt that in the 19th century, many were ground up and sold abroad as fertilizer.

And You Thought You Wanted to Be a Mummy...

Some Buddhist monks in Asia subject their bodies to a slow process of deliberate mummification before death. First, they alter their diet by eliminating rice, barley and beans—all foods that provide a haven for bacteria after death. Next, they drink a special tea brewed from tree sap with properties that dehydrate the body but are also poisonous to the bacteria that attack the body after death. The monks also begin to drink water from a special spring that has been found to contain arsenic, which also kills bacteria. Eventually, the monks cease to eat altogether.

A monk undergoing the process of self-mummification is walled up in a cell toward the end of his life. By this point, he is no longer eating and spends the majority of his time meditating. Meditation helps the mummification process by lessening the body's need for oxygen, and the monk is often surrounded by candles to help in the drying process. Air is pumped into the cell through a tube. The monk rings a bell each day to let those outside know he is still alive. Once the bell stops ringing and the monk is assumed to be dead, the air tube is sealed. The body is left in the cell for 1000 days, after which the cell is opened to see if the mummification worked. Few have been successful.

DID YOU KNOW?

Some well-known political leaders of the 20th century had their bodies mummified, including Argentina's Eva Peron, the Soviet Union's Vladimir Ilyich Lenin and China's Mao Zedong.

Mummy Movies

Been wrapped up in your work lately and just want to spend some quiet time unwinding this Halloween evening? How about grabbing a bowl of popcorn and settling in to watch one of these mummy movies, perfect for a night when the dead are said to roam the earth.

 The Mummy **(1932).** Archeologists discover the mummy of an ancient Egyptian high priest named Imhotep (Boris Karloff). In life, Imhotep had been madly in love with a priestess and princess named Anckesenamon. When she dies, he tries to bring her back from the dead but is thwarted. He is buried alive as punishment for his actions. An archeologist accidentally brings the high priest back to life by reciting the words on an ancient scroll. The movie (and the subsequent sequels) revolve around Imhotep's efforts to locate and revive his long-lost love.

***The Aztec Mummy* (1959).** When an ancient ceremonial mask is stolen from an Aztec temple, the mummy appointed to guard it for all eternity comes to life to hunt down the thief.

 ***The Mummy: The Tomb of the Dragon Emperor* (2008).** Alex O'Connell, son of the famed duo of previous *Mummy* movies, is in China helping on an archeological dig. The expedition is unearthing the tomb of the ancient Emperor Han and his army. A priceless diamond carried to China for the British government by O'Connell's parents (father Rick is played by Brendan Fraser) has the power to wake the evil emperor, who was cursed by the sorceress Zi Yuan. The O'Connells and their friends find themselves in a race to stop the mummy and his army from reaching Shangri La.

A Mummy at the Meeting!

When British philosopher, author and proponent of utilitarianism Jeremy Bentham died on June 6, 1832, he bequeathed his sizeable estate to the newly founded University of London (now University College London). However, his will attached an odd condition to the bequest: his body was to be embalmed, dressed and placed seated in a chair in a glass cabinet, where it was to be forever on display at the institution. As well, it was to be present at the annual meeting of the university administrators.

His wishes were carried out, though an embalming accident made it necessary to replace his real head with a wax replica. (The real one was also put on display between the philosopher's feet until the decision was made to store it elsewhere after it had been stolen several times by student pranksters.) The tradition of wheeling Bentham in his display case into the annual meetings still continues. His presence is noted in the minutes, where he is listed as "not voting."

TOMBSTONE TRIVIA

Graveyards, the final resting places of the dead, are naturally associated with Halloween, the festival of the dead. Graveyards, tombstones and all things connected to death and dying have a place on Halloween. Front yards sport tombstones, and ghosts sway from the branches of trees. This section presents some interesting information and spooky tales on graveyards and the things found in them.

You Can't Keep a Good Man Down— or Can You?

Why do we put tombstones on top of graves? Long ago, people were afraid that the spirits of the dead would leave their resting place to disturb the lives of the people still living. In an attempt to prevent this, a stone was placed on top of a deeply dug grave. As added protection, the lid of the coffin was sometimes nailed shut.

The Witch's Stone of Great Leighs

In Great Leighs, Essex, England, there is a very large "tombstone" in the village green. Legend states that this stone sits on top of the spot where a particularly evil witch was buried in order to keep her from harming the village's inhabitants, even after death.

In June 1944, American troops in Britain were transporting equipment from London down to the coast. One of these conveys made its way to Great Leighs, where it was prevented from going any farther by the large stone on Scrapfaggot Green. The soldiers did not want to turn around and search out another route; they were already making poor time because of the narrow, winding dirt roads. Instead, they decided to move the stone. They put a chain around the two-ton boulder and pulled it out of their way with one of the trucks. Then, they drove on.

Later that day, an old man of the village noticed that the Witch's Stone had been moved. Worried, he hurried to a local pub to spread the news. The next night, strange incidents began to occur in the village. The midnight church bells rang at 2:30 AM instead. Animals were moved to different pastures or from the barn to a field.

Every night, the weird occurrences became more threatening. Animals were no longer moved, but killed. Furniture was thrown about during the night—with no one hearing a sound! People began to stay awake at night to try to catch the perpetrator. No one was ever caught, and no evidence of a hoax was ever found.

Given the increasingly alarming nature of the unusual events, some of the men of the village decided it would be best to return the Witch's Stone back to its former spot over the reputed witch's grave. So they hooked the rock up to a tractor and moved it back. Immediately, the bizarre happenings ceased!

Tombstones Belong on Tombs

Good friend for Jesus sake forbeare,
To dig the dust enclosed here.
Blessed be the man that spares these stones,
And cursed be he that moves my bones.

–William Shakespeare's epitaph at Stratford-upon Avon

It is a long-standing superstition that using old tombstones to construct paths, roads or buildings will result in bad luck. The inhabitants of a building made with these stones will fall victim to misfortune and haunting. People traveling on roads or paths made with old tombstones suffer frequent accidents. Is it possible that there is some basis for this superstition? Read the next two stories and decide for yourself.

Troubled Tombstones

Tenants of a fourplex in Coquitlam, British Columbia, experienced a number of disturbing incidents in 1986: furniture was moved, television channels were switched and a ghost was even seen! The cause of the disturbances was apparently the stones used to build the tenement's walkways. These were no ordinary stones—they were tombstones that had been taken from the cemetery at the Woodlands Hospital! The owner eventually agreed to return the tombstones to their rightful owners. After he did so, the strange occurrences stopped.

Grandpa Tylaska's Tombstone

The Tylaska family live in a home by a Connecticut seaport. The house was built in 1807 by the great-great-great-grandfather of Mrs. Tylaska. When the Tylaskas first moved into the house, they did some renovations to the building, including painting the exterior. It was not long before the ghost of the original builder began appearing around the house. These sightings continued until one day when Mr. Tylaska noticed an unusually shaped stone in the rock wall on the property. Unlike the other stones, this one appeared to have been worked by human hands. Removing it from the pile, he discovered it was the tombstone of his wife's ancestor. Why was it in the wall and not the cemetery?

Inquiries revealed that when a new cemetery had been built in town, the graves from the old family graveyard had been moved, and Mrs. Tylaska's great-great-great-grandfather had received a new tombstone; the old one was discarded. The family decided not to return the tombstone to the rock wall;

instead, they set it up in their backyard and the old man's ghost was never seen again.

Tombstone Tidbits

- Fifteenth- and sixteenth-century grave monuments reveal that people were concerned with the body's corruption after death. An example is the tomb of John Wakeman, a 16th-century bishop of Gloucester. His tomb at Tewkesbury depicts a rotting corpse with a rat, snakes and snails feasting on the decaying flesh.

- The Celts regarded cats as a symbol of death, and thus the image of a cat often appears on tombstones in Celtic areas.

- According to an old English superstition, if a cat is seen lying or sitting on top of a tombstone, it is a sign that the soul of the person buried there is in Hell.

- William Mullen's wife was so fed up with his drinking that when he died in 1863 in Clayton, Alabama, she had his tombstone made to look like a whiskey bottle!

- Tombstone, Arizona, was once one of the roughest, toughest towns of the Wild West. It got its name from the many fatal shootings that occurred there. The town itself eventually died away. Today, it has been given a new lease on life as a tourist attraction. People come to see the place where the legendary gunfight at the OK Corral occurred, pitting Wyatt Earp and Doc Holliday against the Clancy and McLaury Gang. Tourists also come hoping to encounter one of this ghost town's 31 spectral residents.

- Between 1902 and 1949, tombstones could be ordered from the Sears catalog.

 In Mexico, the cross to mark a new grave is kept at home until the next Days of the Dead. Then, it is blessed and placed at the head of the grave.

 A company in Austria sells glow-in-the-dark tombstones.

Creating Your Own Graveyard

For those wanting to turn their front lawn into a graveyard on Halloween, here are some suggestions for tombstone epitaphs:

B. Ware	Justin Pieces
C.U. Soon	Miss N. Cranium
Diane Rott	M.T. Toom
Dusty N. Crumblin	Stella Alive
Frank N. Stein	U.R. Next
I.C. You	Will B. Back
I. Emma Ghost	Will Knott Rest
I.L. Beebach	Xavier Breath
Ima Goner	

Macabre Medicines

Do you know people who turn up their nose when it comes to taking their medicine? Show them this list of early remedies from the graveyard and maybe they won't be so reluctant next time!

- Amulets and rings made from the metal fixings of old coffins have long been believed to prevent cramps, arthritis and rheumatism, especially if blessed by a monarch. Queen Mary I (1553–58) was the last English monarch to bless these charms.

- In early modern England (c. 1550–c. 1750), one treatment for dysentery was to drink red wine mixed with powdered human bones.

- Up until the 19th century in England, epileptics were given ground skull bone in their food as a treatment. If the skull had belonged to a person who had committed suicide, the remedy was thought to be much more effective.

- To prevent cramps, people in England once wore the knuckle bones or patellae of a human or sheep in a pouch around their necks.

- Headache relief could be obtained by driving a nail into a dead person's skull.

- To prevent a miscarriage, walk over the grave of a dead man three times, while each time repeating a short Latin verse.

COFFINS AND CORPSES

Casket Capers

🪦 The folks in Manitou Springs, Colorado, have a unique way of celebrating the Halloween season. Every year on October 31, teams race coffins on wheels down a hill. Each team has five members—the "body" and four "mourners." Prizes are awarded for the fastest coffin, the most creative casket and the best body.

The coffin race commemorates a former resident, spiritualist Emma Crawford. When Emma died in 1890, her body was buried on nearby Red Mountain.

During a 1929 landslide, her coffin was washed down the side of the mountain and into the town! The "bodies" in the racing coffins are dressed up to look like that of Miss Crawford.

Dutch entertainer Eddy Daams has invented a new extreme sport—being buried alive. The participant is buried in a coffin five feet underground for one hour. The coffin is equipped with an oxygen supply, a panic button and a webcam (so friends and family can watch).

At the annual Procession of the Shrouds held during July in Ribarteme, Spain, coffins are paraded through the town. In them lie people who have cheated death the previous year. The parade is an expression of gratitude to God for sparing their lives.

DID YOU KNOW?

The ghost of the Scottish fur trading baron Simon McTavish has been seen on the snowy slopes of Montreal's Mount Royal—he seems to be having fun, riding his coffin down the mountain!

Coffin Curiosities

Roger Fox of Fairborn, Ohio, built a car out of two coffins and parts of other vehicles. He plans to be buried in it.

It was important in Poland that the wood used to make a coffin have no knots because every knot in a coffin meant a child would die.

A casket lined in pink silk traveled everywhere with the French actress Sarah Bernhardt. This was where this famous woman practiced her lines and slept!

Buried Alive!

There was a young man named Nunhead
Who awoke in his coffin of lead,
"It's cosy enough," he remarked in a huff,
"But I wasn't aware I was dead!"

—18th-century limerick

A Common Fear

For centuries, people have feared being buried alive. Prior to the 20th century and modern medicine, it was often impossible for a doctor to determine with certainty whether a person was in fact dead or was simply in a coma or unconscious. As a result, hundreds of people were buried alive—scratch marks inside coffins attest to this horrible end. There are stories of people awakening at their own funeral, of women giving birth while buried alive and of grave robbers finding a living person rather than a corpse in the coffin. Some people insisted on waiting until decomposition began before allowing burial to occur.

Bateson's Belfry

During the 19th century, several methods were developed to lessen the possibility of waking to find oneself buried alive with no way out of the grave. John Bateson developed a special coffin, known as Bateson's Belfry, which was equipped with a bell attached by a string to the hand of the person being buried so the bell could be rung if the person awoke. Bateson never tried out his invention. The man was so scared of the possibility of being buried alive that he did his best to ensure that he was definitely dead before being buried—he doused himself in linseed oil and set himself on fire!

DID YOU KNOW?

The Russian author Nikolai Gogol was scared of being buried alive. It appears he worried with good reason—when his remains were disinterred a few years after his burial in 1852, his body had rolled over in the casket!

Vienna's "New" Morgue

In the 1870s, a new morgue was built in Vienna in which corpses were laid on specially designed "couches" consisting of two metal plates attached to numbered bells. Even the slightest movement of the corpse was supposed to set off the bell. Bodies were kept there until death was assured. Suicides were the only exception as it was deemed unnecessary because they truly desired not to live.

DID YOU KNOW?

The phrase "graveyard shift" is derived from the practice of hiring people to spend the night in the local graveyard listening for the sounds of bells ringing or voices calling from the graves to indicate that someone had accidentally been buried alive.

Burial in the 21st Century

The bodies of the dead have been disposed of in many different ways through the centuries and across the globe. Burial, mummification, cremation and exposure are just some of the more frequently encountered. With the huge technological leaps as well as the changes in social structures in general in the last century, people today have more options than ever before when it comes to choosing what they wish to happen to their own or their loved one's remains. Cemeteries will never look the same again!

Canuck Sportsman's Memorial Company provides a unique distribution service for "cremains"—the ashes are loaded in shotgun shells and shot into the wilderness or at an animal.

Bettye Wilson-Brokl owns and operates a company called Eternally Yours. She incorporates the ashes of a loved one into a painting. The idea came to her when her mother's remains were to be buried in a plot far from where she lived; she wanted to have her mother close to her. Her company offers the option of leaving parts of a painting undone in order to incorporate the ashes of other loved ones when they die.

There is a company in the U.S. that rents space from NASA on probes to the moon that they then sell to people who wish to have their cremains scattered upon the lunar surface.

Mummification is once more an option at some funeral homes. A few mortuary science programs, such as the one at Lynn University in Florida, are teaching students how to mummify the dead.

Some firms are now offering to build custom-designed coffins. You can choose any shape you wish, such as an airplane or ballet shoe, and it will be built to house your body after death.

If you are of a more practical bent, Hans Rademaker of the Netherlands has developed a bookcase that can be turned into a coffin when the owner dies.

Now you can really see the dead come to life! Funeral homes offer a solar-powered video screen to be placed on the grave of your loved one. Complete with headphone jacks, this device can store and play a five-minute video of clips from the life of the deceased.

Several companies now offer to turn cremains into diamonds. Only eight ounces of ashes will yield approximately 10 one-carat diamonds. It takes between three and four months to turn cremains into diamonds—one month to isolate the carbon in the cremains, and one to two months to turn the cremains into a rough gemstone through the application of intense heat and pressure. Finally, an additional month is needed to cut the diamond. All diamonds made from cremains are either yellow or blue in color.

Ghia Gallery of San Francisco creates unique coffins and urns. The resulting resting places are often quirky works of art, such as an egg-carton-shaped urn supported by a dozen chicken legs or a liquor cabinet that plays the tune "How Dry I Am."

Mark Zeabin of Krestova, BC, designs and makes bars, sofa beds, bookshelves and stereo stands that can be converted into coffins.

Beginning in the 1960s, some funeral homes began offering a speedy mourning option for an increasingly fast-paced society. Drive-thru viewings allow mourners to drive up to a window to view the deceased and pay their last respects in a timely fashion.

In Los Angeles, there is a pet cemetery that is just for the virtual pets known as Tamagotchis!

The Florida firm Eternal Ascent Society Inc. sends people's ashes up in a biodegradable balloon. The balloon freezes and breaks at about 5.5 miles up in the air, scattering the deceased's cremains into the wind.

How Do You Say "To Die"?

There are many slang phrases that mean "to die." Because Halloween is a night to honor and remember the dead, it was thought appropriate to list a few of these terms.

- bite the dust
- buy the farm
- cash in your chips
- catch a packet
- check out
- croak
- cross over to the other side
- go to the Happy Hunting Grounds
- kick the bucket
- meet your Maker
- push up daisies
- put on the wooden overcoat
- sleep with Jesus
- sleep with the fishes

THE GRIM REAPER

The Personification of Death

It took many centuries for the figure of death as a Grim Reaper to develop. Beginning with the Black Death (bubonic plague) of the mid-14th century, a skeletal figure carrying a scythe began to appear periodically in European art and literature. The 19th century, with its morbid fascination with all things gothic, witnessed a rapid increase in such depictions. By the 20th century, the Grim Reaper was a widely recognized reminder of people's mortality.

In Art and Literature

☠ A line from an old German folksong went, "There is a reaper, Death by name."

☠ In a procession through the city of Florence in 1433, a figure of Death carried a scythe while riding on a black wagon painted with skulls and bones. Skeletons popped out of spring-loaded graves on the wagon.

☠ Pieter Brueghal's painting, *The Triumph of Death* (c. 1562), depicts death as a skeleton riding an emaciated old horse and carrying a scythe. The landscape is strewn with his victims.

☠ In Shakespeare's *Antony and Cleopatra* (III, 13, 196), Antony speaks of death with "his pestilent scythe."

☠ In Cervantes' *Don Quixote* (1605, Vol. 1; and 1615, Vol. 2), death is referred to as a male reaper.

☠ In Hungary and Romania, the bodies of the dead were often buried with a sickle, which could be used to slay them if they should try to rise from the dead.

☠ The Transylvanians portrayed death as a skeleton holding a sickle or a scythe, while for the eastern Slavs, it was a woman who carried one of these.

☠ In Daniel Chodowiecki's *Dance of Death* collection of 1791, a skeletal death wields a scythe in two scenes—when he cuts down a woman selling fish at the marketplace and when he uses it to knock a soldier off his horse.

☠ The late 18-century German artist Matthias Claudius depicted "Friend Death" as a skeleton with a scythe.

☠ In Columbian folklore, there is a representation of death known as the "scythe woman."

GHOSTLY SKELETONS

Turin's Ghostly Rider

A northern Italian castle near the city of Turin is home to 17 ghostly apparitions. The one most frequently seen is that of a skeletal man riding a skeletal horse along the castle's corridors. The man, known as Arturo, is wearing a cross around his neck. In 1980, the bones of a horse and rider with a metal cross were unearthed in the now dry moat of the castle.

Heavy Collar and the Blackfoot Woman

Heavy Collar was the chief of the tribe of Blood Natives encamped near the Cypress Hills in Alberta, Canada. One day, he led a group of warriors on a raid. However, when they arrived, they discovered that their enemies had been alerted and were long gone. Heavy Collar was frustrated and needed some time to think and work off his anger. He asked his brother-in-law to lead the braves to the Old Man River and set up camp there. Heavy Collar told him he would meet them there eventually.

Heavy Collar then went in search of a buffalo to hunt. After killing and butchering the animal, the chief packed up as much meat as he could carry and began to head in the direction of the river. Tired, he found a soft patch of grass on a hill where he could sleep.

In the morning, Heavy Collar woke up with a start to find the skeleton of a woman curled up beside him. He could tell from the remains of her dress that she had been a member of the Blackfoot tribe. The skeleton turned and addressed him as husband. It seemed that he had accidentally gone to sleep on the same spot she had once died. Seeing all the meat he carried, she decided that he would make a good husband and provider. Alarmed, Heavy Collar grabbed his things and ran. Heavy Collar could sense the skeleton woman chasing him so he fired his gun behind him. He hit his target, who screeched in rage, threatening to harm such a brutal husband.

When the chief returned to camp and told the warriors what had happened, they quickly packed up and headed home. Unfortunately, it was not long before the skeleton woman arrived, seeking revenge. Everyone dashed inside the chief's tent to hide, but the skeleton woman blocked the vent of the tipi so the smoke could not escape. Finally, the chief's mother took out a special peace pipe and left the tipi, hoping to placate the angry spirit. Instead, the skeleton woman sucked the very life right out of the old woman. The skeleton woman's shrieking laughter could be heard departing as Heavy Collar's mother fell over dead.

Libera Nos and Her Skeleton Crew

In the early 1870s, the ship *Libera Nos*, along with its captain Bernard Fokke and all its crew members, vanished while sailing the Pacific. Legend states that Fokke gambled with the Devil and lost. Since its disappearance, the *Libera Nos* has been seen by ships throughout the Pacific. Bathed in a reddish-gold glow, the ship's sails are in tatters. The captain and crew are no more than skeletons dressed in rags. Bad luck has plagued the ships and crews that have witnessed the sudden appearance and then disappearance of this ghost ship. Every German U-boat that saw the *Libera Nos* and its skeletal crew was eventually lost.

The last entry in the captain's logbook for the steamship *Hannah Regan*, which sank off Okinawa in 1899, refers to a sighting of the *Libera Nos*. Even rescue efforts to salvage the gold that sank with the *Hannah Regan* were abandoned after being thwarted by subsequent appearances of the ghost ship and its skeleton crew. With many deaths and much ill fortune attributed to it, the *Libera Nos* still plies the waters of the Pacific today. Who will be unlucky enough to see it next?

A Fisherman's Fright

A fisherman was down by the Nova Scotia shoreline repairing his lobster traps when he saw a figure emerge from the water about 100 yards away. It was no ordinary person, but a ghostly skeleton covered in seaweed. The fisherman watched as the ghost brushed off the seaweed and then turned and walked across the sand toward him. Coming closer, the skeleton suddenly stopped and looked at the fisherman, aware of his presence. Eventually, the skeleton continued on out of sight. Later that day, the fisherman, still mending his lobster traps, watched as the skeleton reappeared from the direction it had gone earlier. It walked past him and back to the spot where it had emerged from its watery grave. Then, just before disappearing into the sea again, it turned and waved goodbye to the stunned fisherman.

An Unsightly Glimpse of the Future

A number of British pilots were gathered in the mess hall at their base in Shallufa, Egypt. It was during World War II, and the men were enjoying a drink before flying out on another mission the next day. At some point during the evening, Wing Commander George Potter glanced across the hall to where another wing commander named Roy sat. When Roy looked over his way, Potter was horrified to see not a man's face, but a skull with bits of flesh dangling from it. Potter read it as a sign that Roy would die during the next day's mission. He was right. Wing Commander Roy never returned.

DID YOU  KNOW?

According to the *Guinness Book of Records*, on September 24, 2009, 197 audience members at The Paul O'Grady Show in London, UK, dressed up as skeletons. This is the largest such gathering on record.

THE EVOLUTION OF HALLOWEEN

"Hallowtide" Before the Reformation

Mention of Halloween (or Hallowmas), All Saints' Day and All Souls' Day appears periodically in various surviving records from before the middle of the 16th century. Some of these appear below:

- A game of bobbing for apples is depicted in the 14-century manuscript, *Luttrell Psalter*.

- *The Book of Ceremonial* for the court of Henry VII (r. 1485–1509) states that on All Saints' Day, the monarch is to wear purple and his attendants black, the colors representing mourning.

- A 1517 Churchwardens' account for Heybridge, Essex, records payments made to Andrew Elyott and John Gidney of Maldon for repairing the clacker and rope of the bell for "Hallowmasse." (Bells were rung through-out the night on Halloween to scare away any evil spirits roaming about that night.)

- In the parish of St. Mary Woolnoth in London, five young, garlanded women were paid to play their harps by candlelight on Halloween in 1539.

- In Bristol, the mayor was expected to entertain the city council on Halloween with bonfires, spiced "cakebread" and wine.

Halloween and the English Reformation

In England, the Reformation led to the banning of Halloween celebrations. Not only were these festivities linked to the pagan past in the minds of churchmen, but the new beliefs concerning death and sin also made such practices redundant. The Catholic Church had taught (and still does) that after death, the soul may go to one of three places—Heaven, Purgatory or Hell. Most souls ended up in Purgatory, a place where they stayed until they had been cleansed of all their sins. While a better alternative to Hell, Purgatory was not a nice place to end up, so most people would offer prays for the souls of departed loved ones (or leave monetary bequests in their wills to have prayers said for their own souls).

The new Protestant tradition taught that Purgatory did not exist. Instead, souls were destined from birth to go either to Hell or to Heaven. There was no point in praying for the souls of the dead because these prayers would have no effect on where a person spent eternity. Thus, the prayers and offerings made for the dead on All Hallows' Eve, All Saints' Day and All Souls' Day were declared unnecessary, un-Protestant and illegal.

However, as is often the case with long-held customs, many people refused to stop practicing their traditions without a fight. Court records from 16th- and 17th-century England are littered with references to the long and painful death of many of these practices. For example, in 1587, the local parson was attacked by men at Hickling in Leicestershire when the parson tried to stop them from ringing the church bells, and a constable in Wellington, Somerset, was accosted by revelers in 1604 when he attempted to stop their seasonal festivities.

Guy Fawkes Day

In 1605, however, an event occurred that English government and church authorities were quick to seize upon as a means of transferring the people's traditional celebrations into a more acceptable, secular holiday. On November 5, a Catholic man named Guy Fawkes was caught under the Parliament buildings with a number of kegs of gunpowder. He and his fellow conspirators had been planning to blow up Parliament that very day. Since then, the English have celebrated Guy Fawkes Day with the bonfires and mischief once reserved for All Hallows' Eve. For example, in Lincolnshire, the practice of tossing stones into the bonfire to divine the future moved from Halloween to Guy Fawkes night.

In the areas of England (such as the north and the west) where many people remained Catholic, the old practices continued for a long time. In 1783, English Catholics lit hilltop bonfires on All Saints' night. In some parts of England in the 18th century, people carried a burning candle through the hills at midnight on Halloween. If it did not go out during this hour, the bearer was protected against witchcraft for another year. Even into the early 20th century, some areas still kept the traditions alive. In Lancashire, Halloween was known as Teanday or Day of Fire. On that day, farmers burned straw on their pitchforks and prayed for the dead.

Reforming Halloween in Scotland

Religious reformers in the 16th century adopted the form of Continental Protestantism established by John Calvin in Switzerland. Over time, this was modified to become the brand of extreme Protestantism known as Presbyterianism. Church leaders in Scotland, like those in neighboring England, forbade the keeping of traditional Halloween customs. However, authorities in Scotland found this prohibition even more difficult to enforce than those in the south because of the treacherous terrain in the northern parts of that country. The resistance of the Scottish people to these new laws was aided by the greater Celtic component in their cultural makeup. In some areas of Scotland, the old Halloween customs never died out and are still being kept today.

- In 1589, the presbytery at Stirling, Scotland, forbade the lighting of "hallowmas fires."

- In 1648, the kirks (churches) at Fife and Slain in Scotland prohibited the lighting of Halloween fires.

- In 1741, an Anglesey writer noted a decline in the number of Halloween bonfires.

- In 18th-century Edinburgh, the Hallowmas fair was a time for courtship, revelry and drinking.

- Thomas Pennant, writing at the end of the 18th century, noted that at sunset on October 31 in the eastern Scottish Highlands, people would run around their villages carrying torches to protect them from witches and fairies the following year.

🔥 In 1840, 30 hilltop bonfires with people dancing around them were seen on Halloween from the short stretch of road between Dunkeld and Aberfeldy.

🔥 Halloween bonfires were common in 19th-century Perthshire.

🔥 In northeastern areas of Scotland in the 19th century, family members carried torches of fir wood around their fields on All Hallows' Eve to protect them in the coming year.

🔥 In 19th-century Corgarff, Scotland, after walking around the fields with torches on All Hallows' Eve, people threw them into a bonfire chanting, "Brave bonfire, burn a, Keep the fairies a awa."

DID YOU KNOW?

In Scotland, Halloween bonfires were once called "shannocks," and October 31 was known as "Shannock Night."

HALLOWEEN: A FESTIVAL OF LOVE?

Prior to the 1930s, Halloween parties were meant for single young people. They were seen as an opportunity for young people to meet, an opportunity for matchmaking. Most of the activities of the evening were designed to bring together young couples or to aid individuals to discover their marital futures.

Between 1875 and 1935, Halloween parties took many forms, including society balls, masquerade parties, barn dances, progressive dinners and bridge socials. These parties and dances usually involved kissing games and mistletoe would be hung. Entertainment often revolved around games of fortune-telling.

While costumes were generally quite simple with most being homemade, decorations were elaborate and food was plentiful. Beautifully colored autumn leaves, corn and pumpkins along with cutouts of black cats and bats were the decorations of choice.

To highlight the difference between the thrills and chills of today's Halloween with the veritable mate market of yesteryear, compare the list of Halloween songs for today found later in this book with the list from the October 1926 edition of *Today's Housewife* magazine: "Love, Will You Marry Me?," "My Sweetheart," "Our Love," "Cupid's Garden," "I Love You Truly" and "Love's Old Sweet Song."

Tam Lin and Jenny

The ancient Celts had tales of love that occurred at Samhain. An old British border ballad tells the tale of a young man named Tam Lin. He goes out riding in the woods one day and is seen by the fairy queen. The queen desires to make Tam Lin her own and so she kidnaps him. Tam Lin, however, already has a human love named Jenny. Jenny wants her beloved back, and she goes into the woods on All Hallows' Eve to rescue him. She waits for the fairy procession, which she knows must pass by. She spots Tam Lin seated upon a white horse, so she grabs him and pulls him off. The fairy queen uses magic to change Tam Lin into numerous terrifying beasts in an attempt to force Jenny to release him. Still, Jenny does not let go. She courageously holds onto her love until dawn and, by doing so, breaks the spell. Tam Lin is able to return to Jenny and the world of humans once more.

Oenghus and Caer

Another tale is about the Celtic god of love and youth, Oenghus mac Oc, who fell in love with a beautiful young maiden named Caer. Caer's father did not approve of the match and did his best to keep the two separate. Caer, however, possessed the ability to turn herself into a white swan each year on the festival of Samhain. Being a god, Oenghus was also able to transform himself into a swan so that he could be together with his beloved without her father knowing. Oenghus then used his powers to put everyone at the festival into a deep sleep that lasted three days and nights in order to allow the two lovers to escape to his palace home.

Party Games from Yesteryear

The Halloween parties of the late 19th and early 20th centuries involved many games designed to bring people together and to playfully provide an atmosphere conducive to love. Bobbing for apples and the many other apple fortune-telling rites were popular. Here is a list of some of the other amusements enjoyed by young adults a century ago:

- The letters of the alphabet were carved on a pumpkin. Guests were blindfolded and then given a hat pin or wand to point at it to discover the initials of their future mate.

- A dozen kernels of popcorn were placed in a wire popper, which was then held over an open flame. The number of kernels that did not pop indicated the number of years before marriage.

- Halloween parties from the first quarter of the 20th century featured table centerpieces known as "Jack Horner Pies." These came in a variety of shapes and forms, but all contained surprise gifts and treats for the guests. Sometimes each guest would reach in and pull out a prize in much the same manner as the boy in the nursery rhyme. Other times, each guest selected a ribbon dangling from the centerpiece and pulled it until the prize came out.

- Single women dripped hot candle wax into a bowl of cold water. The shape of the hardened wax foretold their future. So, for example, bells would indicate a wedding, a cornucopia meant wealth and a torch signified fame.

- A guest would burn a twig in a fire while recounting a ghost story, stopping when the twig had burned completely. Another guest would continue the story.

- A bowl of "crowdie" would be served to guests. Crowdie was a dessert made from whipped cream and spiced applesauce mixed together. In it were buried rings, marbles and coins. Guests who got a helping with a ring in it would be married in the near future, while those who ended up with a marble were destined to remain single. Those who found a coin would become rich.

Grulacks and Their Gals

On Halloween, on the Shetland Islands, groups of costumed young men known as Grulacks went from house to house offering song and dance in exchange for food. On the following night, these young men would invite a group of single women to join them for a party at which the collected food was consumed.

DID YOU  KNOW?

In Victorian England, it was popular to conduct a family séance on Halloween.

THE TIME OF THE WITCH TRIALS

Scared of the witches that prowl the streets on Halloween every year? So were many Europeans who lived during the centuries of the witchcraze.

Europe's Big Witch Hunt

For approximately 300 years, between 1450 and 1750, Europeans executed people for practicing witchcraft. During this time, scholars estimate that around 100,000 people died, directly or indirectly, from an accusation of witchcraft. Of these, about 80 percent were women, often old widows. (Interestingly, in some areas, alleged witches were almost exclusively men—for example, in Iceland, Russia and Scandinavia.)

A belief in magic was nothing new. The term "witch" comes from the old Saxon term for "wise one": *wicce* for a woman, *wicca* for a man. Such people were both respected and feared; they were respected because their knowledge allowed them to do beneficial things such as cure the sick, yet feared because they were also able to use that information to harm others if they so chose. Nonetheless, being a witch was not considered to be a horrible, scary thing as long as it was believed that only people or their property was being hurt. However, when the Church declared a link between witchcraft and Satanism by also trying people accused of sorcery with the crime of heresy, witchcraft came to seen as distinctly evil because it was now perceived as jeopardizing a person's soul.

The first trials for witchcraft occurred in the German-speaking areas of the Holy Roman Empire in the middle of the 15th century, spreading from there throughout much of Europe and even into the American colonies. The number of trials in any area seems to have followed an alternating pattern with periods of numerous trials and executions followed by only occasional ones. On the European continent and in Scotland, condemned witches were executed by being burned alive. In England, such punishment was reserved for those who committed crimes against the monarch, and thus witches there were hanged.

People accused of being witches in England were usually said to have harmed children through possession or by making them ill or killing them. Scottish and English trials often involved a search for the "witch's mark"—a skin blemish said to be the site where the Devil or demons fed off the witch's blood.

The trials of those charged with witchcraft in German-speaking areas generally focused on the accused witch's supposed interactions with the Devil and his minions.

> *Fillet of a fenny snake,*
> *In the cauldron boil and bake;*
> *Eye of newt, and toe of frog,*
> *Adder's fork and blind-worm's sting,*
> *Lizard's leg, and owlet's wing,*
> *For a charm of powerful trouble,*
> *Like a hell-broth boil and bubble.*
> *Double, double toil and trouble;*
> *Fire burn, and cauldron bubble.*
>
> –William Shakespeare, *Macbeth*

Well-to-do Witches

When we think of the people accused of witchcraft during the period of the European witch hunts, most of us picture poor, elderly widows. Although it is true that many of those accused of being witches were women—and many were poor, elderly widows—men and children were also charged with witchcraft. Indeed, not even those in positions of wealth and power, who are usually immune from legal charges, escaped. Members of the gentry and aristocracy as well as members of both civic and ecclesiastical government faced such accusations, and some were convicted, and even executed, as a result.

> *Sorcerers or witches are the*
> *Devil's whores who steal milk,*
> *raise storms, ride on goats or*
> *broomsticks, lame or maim people,*
> *torture babies in their cradle,*
> *change things into different shapes.*

–Martin Luther, 1521

In Ireland

One of the earliest known trials for witchcraft was that of a wealthy Irish woman named Lady Alice Kyteler. In 1324, she faced numerous charges, including poisoning her fourth husband, denying the power of Christ and the Church, seeking the aid of demons and consorting with an incubus. Lady Alice escaped the charges, fleeing first to Dublin and then to England. However, her maid, Petronilla, was captured and tortured until she confessed. She was burned at the stake.

In England

Nearly 100 years later, in 1419, the English king Henry V prosecuted his stepmother Joan of Navarre for attempting to bring about his death through witchcraft. Later, his son, King Henry VI, accused Eleanor Cobham, Duchess of Gloucester, his aunt-by-marriage, of necromancy, witchcraft, heresy and treason. She was convicted and spent the remainder of her life imprisoned in Leeds Castle.

In France

In 1438, the French knight Pierre Vallin of La Tour du Pin was accused of witchcraft. Under torture, he confessed to being a witch and a follower of the demon Bezlebut for 63 years. He also confessed to flying to witches' sabbats on a stick and to eating children alive there. He was found guilty and executed.

In Scotland

A number of Scottish nobles were the subjects of witchcraft trials in the 16th century. Janet Douglas (Lady Campbell) was the unfortunate victim of a deadly political battle. She was burned at the stake on July 17, 1537, having been convicted of trumped-up charges of witchcraft.

Another Scottish noblewoman, Catherine Rose (Lady Fowllis) was charged with witchcraft in 1560. She was accused of making clay effigies of her husband and Marjory Campbell (Lady Balnagowan), whom she was suspected of attempting to murder. She supposedly shot "elf arrows" (prehistoric arrowheads) at them in an attempt to eliminate them and clear the way for a marriage between Lady Balnagowan's husband and herself.

Euphemia McLean was the daughter of Lord Cliftonhall and the wife of wealthy Patrick Moscrop. She was also a rich woman in her own right. The accusations made against her included the use of magic to capsize a boat and drown 60 people, the attempted murder of her husband in order to marry another man and the attempted murder of the king, in a conspiracy with other witches, through the use of a wax effigy. King James VI, a strong believer in the existence of witches, insisted on her guilt. She was burned at the stake on

July 25, 1591, and her lands were confiscated by the Crown. An act of Parliament the following year enabled her children to retain the remainder of her estate.

The Earl of Bothwell was one of those accused with using witchcraft to try to kill the Scottish king, James VI, in 1592. Bothwell was a reputed necromancer and a known enemy of the king. The actual charge against him was high treason. He was imprisoned in Edinburgh Castle but eventually escaped.

Keeping Away Witches in Scotland

Of all the people in the British Isles, it is the Scots whose history, legends and folk traditions are the most liberally sprinkled with a belief in witches and their propensity to harm others. Scotland was the only country in the British Isles where witches were burned at the stake during the witch hunts of the 16th and 17th centuries. More people were condemned as witches in Scotland than in the more populous country of England. One Scottish king, James VII, even wrote a book in 1597 about witches, entitled *Demonology*.

At Halloween, the people of Scotland were especially careful to protect themselves from the witches believed to be about that night. Farmers would walk backwards around their fields carrying torches to protect the fields and the coming year's crops. Many farmers, not only in Scotland, but also in Wales and Ireland, would light the hay in their pitchforks on fire and wave them in the air to burn the brooms of any witches passing by on their way to their wicked Halloween celebrations with the "Auld Clootie" (the Devil). It was commonly rumored that, as part of these evil festivities, the witches would play music on bagpipes made from the tails of cats and the heads of chickens.

Among the Scottish Highlanders, there was a custom of burning an effigy of a witch on Halloween. This tradition was known as "samhnagen" while the effigy itself was called the "Shandy Dann." The children of Aberdeenshire would collect fuel for the bonfire from the people of the area, crying out, "Give us peet [peat] to burn the witches!" On the night of Halloween, a man dressed as a ghost would deliver the "witch" by horse and cart to the bonfire. This custom was performed in 1874 for Queen Victoria and her family on their Balmoral Castle estate; the queen is said to have greatly enjoyed it. After the "witch" was burned, the people danced and sang and feasted on special Halloween fare. The fire was kept burning long into the night to keep away evil spirits and to burn the brooms of any witches that passed that way.

In the Holy Roman Empire

In the late 16th century, the German noblewoman Agatha von Sontheim zu Nellingsheim was accused of witchcraft. Her Protestant family saved her from prosecution by restoring the territories they ruled to Catholicism and paying a fine of 10,000 gulden.

During the massive witch hunt in Bamberg during the 1620s, many civic leaders were executed, including Johannes Junius, the mayor. Junius was executed as a witch in 1628, but not until he had presided as a judge over the trials of many other accused witches. Shortly before he died, he wrote a letter to his daughter and had it smuggled out of the prison. In it, he stated his innocence and claimed to have only confessed to avoid being tortured further. At this same time, the witch trials in Offenburg claimed the lives of most of the wives and daughters of the town's civic leaders. Likewise, in Oberkirch, many of the community's leading members were burned at the stake.

In New England

During the Salem, Massachusetts, witch trials of 1692, one of the things that led to the eventual end of the hysteria was the accusation of Lady Phips, the wife of Governor William Phips, of being a witch. The accusation of high-ranking members of a community during a period of trials for witch-craft often led to a swift end to the panic. However, this was not always the case: sometimes the hunters found themselves the hunted as was seen in the case of Mayor Junius.

The Condemned "Witches" of Salem, 1692

Hanged June 10
Bridget Bishop

Hanged July 19
Sarah Good
Elizabeth How
Susanna Martin
Rebecca Nurse
Sarah Wilds

Hanged August 19
Rev. George Burroughs
Martha Carrier
George Jacobs
John Proctor
John Willard

Convicted September 6
Mary Bradbury (escaped)
Sara Cloyce (reprieved)
Rebecca Eames (reprieved)
Dorcas Hoar (reprieved)
Abigail Hobbs (reprieved)
Mary Lacy (reprieved)

Pressed to Death September 19
Giles Cory

Hanged September 22
Martha Cory
Mary Esty
Alice Parker
Mary Parker
Ann Pudeator
Wilmot Reed
Margaret Scott
Samuel Wardwell

Convicted, Pleaded Pregnancy and Later Released
Abigail Faulkner
Elizabeth Proctor

Died in Jail
Ann Foster
Sara Osbourne

DID YOU KNOW?

Tituba, a slave, was one of the first people accused of witch-craft in Salem and the first to confess. She spent 13 months in jail before being bought from her owner, the Reverend Samuel Parris, and released.

INFAMOUS WITCH HUNTERS

Sweet Revenge

The French attorney general Nicholas Remy (d. 1612) became a demonologist following the death of his infant son after he was cursed by a beggar woman to whom he had not given any alms. She was the first of over 900 people Remy prosecuted and had executed as witches in Lorraine over the next 50 years.

Witches, Witches Everywhere

Pierre de Lancre, a French judge, boasted of executing 600 people between 1608 and 1610 in the Basque-speaking region of Pays de Labourd. He was commissioned by King Henri IV to investigate allegations of the widespread practice of witchcraft in the region. De Lancre concluded that nearly every person living in the area was a practicing witch. He also wrote a number of books on the topics of witches, demons and sorcery.

The Witch Bishop

Gottfried Johann Georg II Fuchs von Dornheim of Bamberg, Germany, was known as the "Witch Bishop" for the horrendous witch hunt he conducted between 1623 and 1633. In 1627, he had a special prison built for those accused of witchcraft. It was called the Witch House and contained both torture chambers and cells, the walls of which were covered in scriptural passages.

The Witch Bishop had at least 600 people tortured and burned as witches. In the process, he made a fortune collecting the confiscated estates of those whom he had executed for witchcraft.

Many people profited from the trials and executions of witches. Convicted witches had their estates confiscated; the money was used to cover the expenses of their trial, incarceration and execution, with the remainder going to the judges and accusers. Others also profited, from innkeepers who housed trial and execution spectators to the people of the town. Johannesburg Castle in Aschaffenburg, Germany, was built between 1607 and 1614 and was paid for entirely by the confiscated estates of those executed for witchcraft.

Philipp Adolf von Ehrenberg of Würzberg

The Witch Bishop's cousin, Prince-Bishop Philipp Adolf von Ehrenberg of Würzberg, terrorized the residents of that state between 1623 and 1631. He was responsible for the deaths of 900 people accused of witchcraft, including 300 children aged four or younger and his own heir, Ernest von Ehrenberg.

The Witchfinder General

Between 1645 and 1647, Matthew Hopkins, England's self-styled "Witchfinder General," traveled around southeastern England trying people for witchcraft. Although torture was not allowed in English witchcraft cases, Hopkins cunningly employed less extreme but no less effective methods, such as sleep deprivation. Others were pricked with a needle so many times in an attempt to identify a witch's mark that they, too, sometimes succumbed to the pain and humiliation and confessed. In all, England's Witchfinder General condemned at least 230 people to death as witches.

Interesting Witch Tidbits

- Over half of all executions for witchcraft occurred in the German-speaking areas of the Holy Roman Empire.

- The first law against witchcraft in England was made in 1563.

- In 1563, the German physician Johann Weyer published the first significant work refuting the existence of witches.

- In the abbey territory of Obermachtel, seven percent of the populace was executed for witchcraft in a three-year period in the 1580s.

- Essex was known as "The Witch County" because more witchcraft trials occurred there than anywhere else in England.

- In 1596, Maria Holin of Nordlingen maintained her innocence despite being subjected to 56 separate applications of torture.

- In London, a rooster once stood trial for being a witch's familiar (demon in disguise).

- A Bavarian law code of 1611 condemned 52 different types of sorcery, witchcraft and superstitions.

- The largest mass witchcraft hysteria occurred in the city of Ellwanger between 1611 and 1618, when 390 people were executed.

- Only seven people were ever executed for witchcraft in Portugal.

- Prosecution for witchcraft was abolished in England in 1726.

Witch Boxes, Bottles and Balls

In the 16th and 17th centuries, witch boxes were popular in England. They contained items that were believed to protect against witchcraft and had protective spells cast upon them.

Witch bottles were charms that protected against witchcraft and countered it. They were first used in Elizabethan England, especially East Anglia, and were particularly popular between the mid-17th and mid-18th centuries. They can still be found in use in some parts of the southern U.S. today.

Witch bottles were often blue or green and no more than three inches in length. Longer ones of gray or brown were known as Greybeards or Bellarmines, named after an infamous Catholic inquisitor. These were glazed with salt, which supposedly wards off evil, and embossed with scary faces. The bottles were also believed to be effective protection against the evil eye. Occasionally, an ordinary bottle was used.

These bottles were hung in chimneys and over doors and windows to prevent witches from entering. To counteract a spell, another witch or a cunning person would place some hair, nail clippings or urine from the victim along with other objects into a witch bottle and seal it. Then, the bottle was either buried in the hearth or doorway or smashed in the fire. Either way, the spell would be broken. If the bottle was buried, the witch would undergo great discomfort, but if it was broken in the fire, the witch would die. If the buried bottle contained urine, it rendered the witch unable to urinate, and her resulting discomfort revealed her identity to her neighbors.

From the 18th century onward, "witch balls" were also hung in windows in England to ward off witches. These glass balls were generally blue or green in color and measured up to seven inches in diameter. By the 19th century, the custom had made its way to the U.S.

Witch Bottle Found Intact

In 2000, an intact witch bottle, dated to 1720, was discovered beneath a house in Reigate, Surrey, England. It had been buried upside down. Subsequent examination revealed that the bottle contained nine bent brass pins; wool, linen and cotton threads; both animal and human hairs; the leg of an insect; a blade of grass; and human urine. The presence of the bent pins and urine is believed to have been intended to make it painful for the witch to urinate.

Identifying Witches

To protect oneself against a "wicked witch" in the early-modern period (c. 1550–c. 1750), a person first had to identify the witch. There were several folk beliefs to guide the individual in such an endeavor. For example, witches were said to be unable to cry. They were also believed by many to have red hair. Other methods used to detect whether or not your neighbor was a witch included the following:

- Cut an elder tree. If it bleeds, it is really a witch in disguise.

- Find a forked branch from a hazelnut tree and use it like a water dowsing rod. It will automatically point at anyone who is a witch.

- Offer a suspected witch some well-salted meat. If the person avoids eating it, he or she is a witch because witches cannot stand to eat salt.

Protection Against Witches

There were many methods that people used to protect themselves and their families from the numerous witches they imagined to be living secretly in their midst. If you are scared of witches and feel the need to protect yourself this Halloween, here are some methods popularly employed by our ancestors that you may want to try:

- Keep a crucifix handy or make the sign of the cross if threatened.

- Wear amber, sardonyx or cat's-eye jewelry.

- Sleep with holy bread under your pillow.

- Keep clover or holly about your house.

- Plant mountain ash, juniper and bay trees around your house.

- Cut a witch; it deprives the witch of power.

- Decorate a tree or bush in front of your house with numerous blown eggs (an Ozark custom).

- Paint a hex sign over the door to your home. (This technique is still frequently used by the Pennsylvania Dutch.)

- Place an iron knife under your doormat. A brass implement will also do the trick.

- Place a knife in a bowl of water and keep it in the entranceway to your house. A witch looking in the bowl will flee, believing that his or her soul has been pierced by the knife (an Aztec custom).

DID YOU  **KNOW?**

Numerous herbs, including vervain, fennel and rosemary, were thought to be effective charms against witchcraft.

Witches in the Movies

The Conqueror Worm **(1968).** This movie is based on Edgar Allan Poe's book of the same name. It is a fictionalized account of the witch hunt conducted by England's self-styled "Witchfinder General," Matthew Hopkins (Vincent Price), in the 1640s.

Bedknobs and Broomsticks **(1971).** In this Disney classic, set during World War II, two London school children are sent to live with an old aunt (Angela Lansbury) in the countryside to escape the nightly German bombings of the city. The children discover that their aunt is an apprentice witch. The movie is an amusing account of her mastery of her new skills and her efforts to use them for her country's benefit.

The Witches **(1990).** A young boy and his grandmother are vacationing at a seaside resort in England. A witches' convention is also being held at the hotel. (Angelica Huston plays the Grand High Witch.) The boy discovers that the witches are planning to rid the world of children. Even after they turn him into a mouse, he tries to stop their wicked plot.

***The Craft* (1996).** Sarah, the new kid at school, has just moved to Los Angeles. She is a hereditary witch, though she is not aware of this until late in the movie. She is befriended by a trio of social outcasts and wannabe witches. The four girls research Wiccan rituals at a local occult store, and Sarah's three friends acquire supernatural powers. The girls use their powers to get revenge on the mean kids at school. Things get out of hand, however, when the vengeance of one girl takes a murderous turn.

 ***The Blair Witch Project* (1999).** Three film students hike into the Black Hills near Burkittsville, Maryland, to shoot a documentary about a local legend known as "The Blair Witch," but the trio never returns. One year later, their video camera is found. The movie allegedly shows the trio's last days and their encounter with evil as revealed on the discovered footage. The movie is shot like an amateur film.

Witches in Stitches

What do you call twin witches?
Double trouble!

What are witches best at in school?
Spelling!

What do you call a witch at the beach?
A sand-witch!

Witches and Black Cats

Witches and black cats have long been associated in popular culture. In the late Middle Ages, the Catholic Church denounced black cats as servants of Satan. Not long afterward, the belief that witches were worshippers of the Devil became widespread. Indeed, Satan and his demon minions were said to often appear to witches disguised as black cats. Lady Alice Kyteler, the first person tried for witchcraft in Ireland (1324), was charged with having sexual relations with a demon, which was said to have appeared to her in a variety of forms, including that of a black cat. Ursula Kempe, a midwife from St. Osyth in Essex, confessed in 1582 to having numerous animal familiars, including a black cat named Jacke.

Another long-held belief was that witches had the ability to turn themselves into black cats. Some believed that a witch's ability to do so was limited to nine times, presumably because a cat was said to have nine lives. This belief was still prevalent in the 19th century, as the next two incidents reveal.

The Cloughfoot Crone

In about 1840, there lived near Cloughfoot Bridge in Lancashire an old woman named Sally Walton who was rumored to be a witch. One night, her neighbor awoke to find a black cat sitting on the foot of his bed staring at him. The farmer chased it away with a knife that he kept on a table near his bed, cutting one of its front legs. The next day, Old Woman Walton had one of her arms wrapped in a kerchief. Everyone in the village believed that the farmer had injured her while she had been transformed into a black cat.

The Eerie Ear

The Reverend Wentworth Webster wrote of an incident that occurred in the Labourd district in France in 1873–74. One night, around midnight, a farmer caught a black cat that he believed was bewitching his cattle and making them ill. He cut off one of the cat's ears to deprive it of its power. (In Normandy, the ears of black cats were removed to prevent them from attending the sabbats.) In the morning, the farmer discovered that the cat's ear had changed into that of a woman's, with an earring! Webster was told that the ear could be seen on display in the town hall.

Which Witch?

It was also commonly thought that black cats were able to become witches. Some medieval people believed that after seven years of service to a witch, a black cat would turn into a witch.

DID YOU  KNOW?

The *chordewa* is a type of witch in the folk traditions of the Bengali Oraon hill tribe. Chordewas are thought to be able to turn themselves into black vampire cats.

BLACK CATS

Fluctuating Feline Fortunes

Nowadays, black cats automatically bring to mind thoughts of ill luck and witches. Their glowing eyes can be found staring menacingly at trick-or-treaters and partygoers on the last day of October every year. Often, they are in the company of their owner, a witch. However, this association with darkness and misfortune has not always been the burden of the black cat.

For black cats (and every other color of feline), ancient Egypt was definitely the time and place to live. Being the adored pet of the goddess Bastet meant that pretty much everyone else treated cats like royalty, especially those people hoping to get in good with its divine owner. Following a life of pampering, after a cat died, its body was mummified so that it could continue its cushy little existence in the afterlife.

Unfortunately for black cats, however, they had their heyday quite early in human history, and since then it has basically been downhill (not straight down, but no bump has ever come close to the glory days of ancient Egypt). Indeed, in medieval Europe, the fortunes of these dark-colored kitties suffered a complete reversal. Their dark color led to associations with the Devil, and their stealthy natures created links in the minds of many with powerful and feared evil witches and, as mentioned earlier, some even believed that black cats were really witches in disguise.

The papal bull of Gregory IX (*Vox in Rama*, 1233) denounced black cats as creatures of the Devil. To rid themselves of these "dangerous" beings, medieval people captured them and trapped them in wicker cages that were then placed in bonfires on Halloween, roasting the poor creatures alive.

Cats with a bit of white fur were saved such a horrific death—the white was thought to be a sign of good and called "the mark of the angel" or "the finger of God."

Today, many people have black cats as pets. As pets, most lead pretty good lives—not quite the pampered princes and princesses of the Egyptian past, but they certainly have nothing to complain about.

Cat Chuckle
What do you get when you cross a black cat with a lemon?
A sour-puss!

Beware of Black Cats

- In Germany, a black cat lying on a grave means that the soul of the deceased belonged to the Devil.

- If a black cat crosses your path from left to right, it signifies good luck. If it crosses from right to left, it foretells bad luck.

- In Italy and Germany, it is said that if a black cat settles on the bed of a sick person, it means the person is going to die.

- In China, encountering a black cat is a sign of impending famine.

- In Ireland, if a black cat crosses your path in the moonlight, it foretells your death in an epidemic.

- In North America, Ireland, Belgium and Spain, it is thought to be unlucky to let a black cat cross your path.

- A saying from the Ozark Mountains in the U.S. warns young women against owning a black cat or they will never find a husband.

- A folk belief from North Carolina states that if a black cat appears when a person dies, it means someone present will also die within the year.

- In Turkey, it is said that if a black cat walks between two people, they will soon quarrel. To prevent this from happening, throw water where the cat walked.

- Russians cautioned that black cats were demons in disguise and should never be allowed to remain indoors during a storm lest the Prophet Elijah strike the building with lightning, setting it on fire.

Twelve Great Black Cats and the Red One

Every Scotsman knows that it is bad luck to go fishing on Halloween when the souls of the dead sail the waves. Murdo MacTaggart did not believe such nonsense and went out fishing on Halloween anyway. Not long after MacTaggart headed out on the open water, a storm blew up. He was forced to return to shore and seek shelter in a hut. Not long afterward, 12 black cats and one red cat came to the hut and demanded payment from MacTaggart for the use of the building. MacTaggart gave them a sheep belonging to the local laird. The cats left, only to return and demand more.

This time, MacTaggart offered them the laird's cow. They took it and went, then returned again for more. This time, he offered them the laird's hound. As the cats went in pursuit of the dog, MacTaggart fled the hut. Hearing the cats returning, he climbed a tree. The red cat spotted him and sent three of the black cats up to get him, but MacTaggart killed them with a knife. The red cat and the nine remaining black ones set about chewing through the tree's roots. MacTaggart screamed for help and was heard by a local minister and his parishioners. They came running, and the minister rescued the fisherman by throwing holy water on the cats. The black cats disappeared, leaving only their skins behind. The red cat transformed into the Devil before also vanishing. MacTaggart vowed that he would never go fishing on Halloween ever again.

Phantom Felines

The word "ghost" usually conjures up images of spectral human beings. Nonetheless, any living being can also exist in spirit form. Several reported ghosts are actually feline phantoms. For example, one of the spirits said to haunt Pengersick Castle in Cornwall is that of Alexander, a black cat that chases ghostly rats around the castle's grounds.

Killakee's Hell Cat

Killakee House in Dublin is said to have been haunted by a scary ghost known as "The Black Cat of Killakee." It had fiery red eyes that stared menacingly at anyone it encountered, scaring them thoroughly. In 1968, the cat disappeared after the building was exorcised, only to return again a year later, after some actors held a séance in the building.

Some believed this spectral cat to be the ghost of a cat burned alive by the notorious 18th-century Hell Fire Club, whose members once met in Killakee House. This was a licentious group led by the wealthy Richard "Burnchapel" Whaley. The group was reputed to have committed numerous atrocities, including the beating death of a poor, deformed boy. Such a skeleton was indeed discovered under the kitchen floor of the building. After it was given a proper burial by a priest, the haunting stopped. Today, a painting of the black cat still hangs in the restaurant; it was painted by Tom McCassey, who is reputed to have seen the cat.

Odd Occurrences at Oxenby

Another spectral cat tale was told by a woman named Mrs. Hartnoll. The frightening encounters had occurred at her childhood home, Oxenby Manor. It was a large, old house, dating back to the 15th century. Above the front entrance was an image of a cat made from black shingles with white-shingle eyes that glowed eerily on moonlit nights. Mrs. Hartnoll's family occupied only the newest wing of the house. When Mrs. Hartnoll was a child, she sometimes sneaked into the older wing to explore. It was there that she had a number of unsettling experiences, including the sensation of an evil presence and the sight of a deformed, malicious-looking man. However, on three separate occasions, she also saw the ghost of a maltreated black cat in its death throes. On each occasion when she saw the cat, a member of her family died later in the day—her brother in an accident, two years later her mother of an epileptic fit, and four years later her father of a heart attack.

Later residents of Oxenby Manor, a Mr. and Mrs. Wheeler, encountered the ghost of a cat, as well. They, their guests and the servants had also seen the ghosts of the ugly man in medieval clothing and the maimed black cat (though there is no mention of these cat sightings immediately preceding a death).

Local legend states that the knight and his lady who once owned the premises were killed while hunting. Their young son was made a ward of the Crown. His guardian was a mean man who abused the boy and tortured his pet cat, killing them both. He then attempted to pass off his own illegitimate son as his ward but was discovered. Both father and son were hanged for the murder. A later owner of the building is said to have added the image of the black cat above the front door in memory of this poor feline.

Creepy Cat Cures

Curiously, although black cats were linked with witches, the Devil and evil in general, they were also a common ingredient in many medieval medicines!

- To avoid sickness in general, it was a good idea to bury the tail of a black cat outside your door.

- A medieval French cure for blindness was to take the ashes from the head of a black cat that had been burned alive and blow them into the eyes of the blind person three times a day until cured.

- Blood from the tail of a black cat was believed to cure shingles if rubbed on the afflicted part.

- A widespread cure for a sty was to rub the tail of a black cat across it. However, in Cornwall, the formula was more complicated. Only a single hair from a black cat's tail was needed—but it had to be pulled from the cat's tail when the new moon rose following a cloudless day! The hair was then stroked across the sty nine times.

- Colonists in North America once thought that tuberculosis could be cured by drinking a broth made by boiling a black cat.

The Christian scholar and theologian Albertus Magnus wrote that to become invisible, it was necessary to boil a black cat's ear in a black sow's milk and then wear it on your thumb!

RATS

Revenge of the Rats

If you go into a store at Halloween, you will probably see a lot of beady little rodent eyes staring menacingly at you. Rats are an increasingly popular decoration inside and outside homes on Halloween. These creatures have a long history in Western cultures of being associated with disease, death and decay.

- Rats often appear in medieval legends as bearing the souls of the dead, who are seeking retributive justice. For example, a Scandinavian legend tells how a swarm of rats killed Earl Asbjorn for murdering St. Knut at Odense in 1086.

- The Polish king Popiel II and his wife are said to have been eaten by rats after years of misrule, culminating in the poisoning of the king's 12 uncles. Bishop Hatto of Mayence is another cruel individual said to have fallen victim to rats. In his case, it was for burning to death a barn full of starving people.

- The 1971 movie *Willard* is based upon this notion of rats executing just vengeance. The title character is a quiet guy who is picked on by everyone—his co-workers, his boss and his mother. His only "friends" are a group of rats that he trains to attack his enemies until the rodents eventually turn against him.

BEWARE OF BATS

"Bat" to the Bone

Thanks to Hollywood's version of Bram Stoker's tale about a blood-sucking vampire in which Dracula is given the power to transform into a bat, this flying mammal has become associated with Halloween. A long tradition as a portent of death or bad luck has also made this homely little creature a natural symbol for this scary festival.

- In England, a bat is an omen of evil (usually of death).

- In Belgium, a bat in the chimney foretells misfortune.

- In North Carolina, a bat flying into the house means that someone in the household will soon die.

- A folk belief from Nova Scotia claims that if a bat flies into a house and lands, a male member of the family will soon die.

🦇 Sicilians believed that bats were incarnations of the Devil come to spy on them and should be burned or hanged alive.

"Bat" Luck

🦇 It is considered bad luck to kill a bat.

🦇 A bat in a house or flying around it three times means that someone who lives there will die soon.

🦇 The Scots believed that a bat that flies straight up and then down was a sign that witches had come for those without charms or other protection from them.

🦇 A bat flying near you means that someone has tried to use witchcraft against you.

🦇 If a bat flies close to you, it is a sign that someone is taking advantage of you.

🦇 Bats were thought to foretell ill luck, and so to protect against this, children would chant:

> *Airy mouse, airy mouse, fly over my head,*
> *And you shall have a crust of bread,*
> *And when I brew and when I bake,*
> *You shall have a piece of my wedding cake.*

People Gone Batty

In the 1974 movie, *The Bat People*, John Beck, a scientist who studies bats, takes his new wife, Cathy, spelunking in Carlsbad Caverns. While in the cave, John is bitten by a bat. Shortly thereafter, he starts hallucinating, and people begin dying. John slowly transforms into a vampire bat, and Cathy is infected by her husband.

Vampire Bats

Bats have a long association with death in many cultures. Vampire bats are especially feared because of their predilection for biting animals and people and drinking their blood. Think of the following curious facts when you see figurines of these "flying rats" decorating buildings next Halloween.

- Every day, vampire bats drink half their body weight in blood.

- While vampire bats are lapping up their daily dose of blood, they are peeing the whole time.

- If a vampire bat is sick, another bat will go and fill up on blood, then return to the cave and vomit it up for its sick comrade to eat.

- The saliva of vampire bats contains a substance called "draculin" that prevents blood from clotting.

- There are three types of vampire bats: common, hairy-legged and white-winged.

- Central and South America are the only places where vampires bats are found.

- Vampire bats have a heat sensor above their nose to help locate the warm areas where blood flows closest to the skin's surface.

- If it goes more than two or three days without eating blood, a vampire bat will die.

- Whenever Catholic Mayans and their animals suffer too much from the bites of vampire bats, they capture one, perform a mass over it, ask it to stop bothering them (and to convey this request to its buddies) and then release it.

Bats in Native American Mythology

- Zotz, the Mayan god of the Underworld, had the head of a vampire bat and was often depicted carrying a bleeding heart.

- For the Moche people, the bat was a symbol of human sacrifice.

- Bats often appeared on the funerary art of the Zapotecs.

- In Mayan art, bats are often shown in conjunction with human bones and skulls.

- The Mayan Hero Twins, Hunahpu and Xbalanque, contended with knife-snouted bats when they went up against the gods of the Underworld. The bats fooled Hunahpu into thinking it was daytime by remaining still for a while. When Hunahpu looked up, they decapitated him. Then Xbalanque fashioned his brother a new head from a pumpkin.

- In the 1930s, the Cakchiquel Maya believed that vampire bats resided in the Underworld, which they left every night to collect blood to make food for their master, the Devil.

OWLS

Now the wasted brands do glow,
Whilst the screech-owl, screeching loud,
Puts the wretch, that lies in woe,
In remembrance of a shroud.

–William Shakespeare, *A Midsummer Night's Dream*
(Act V, Scene 1)

Death by Owl

Since ancient times, people all over the world have believed that the owl was a harbinger of death, and it is this association that has made the owl a symbol of a holiday that honors the dead.

 The Greeks and Romans both thought the sight of an owl at night signified the death of a member of the household. The Romans even held it to be bad luck to see an owl during the day. The Roman scholar Pliny the Elder spoke of the "funereal owl and monster of the night." The deaths of the famous Romans Julius Caesar, Augustus and Agrippa were all said to have been preceded by the hooting of an owl.

Of the many portents of death, the ancient Chinese held the sight of a great horned owl to be the most significant.

Europeans of the 16th century still believed the owl to be a sign of death or bad luck; to avoid these consequences, a person was to quickly turn out his or her pockets and toss some salt into a fire.

Many Native American peoples connected the presence of an owl with impending death. The Cherokee thought of the owl as a messenger of death while the Tsimshian of the Pacific Northwest believed the dead became owls. Among the Kiowa, it was only the deceased shamans who took the form of an owl. The Navaho were of the opinion that ghosts took the form of owls. Dzonokwa, Kwakwaka'wakw goddess of death and rebirth, is associated with the owl and is said to make the same sound as an owl. Members of both the Kwakwaka'wakw and Nootka tribes still say, "I heard the owl call my name," when death is near.

To anyone who has ever heard an owl hoot in the darkness or seen one of these big-eyed birds swoop down on a starry night sky, it is easy to understand why so many people in history have felt a shiver of fear and a sense of doom when this happened. The cry of the owl does sound like one imagines the screams of the damned to sound. One type of North American owl (the small flammulated owl) can throw it voice like a ventriloquist—

now that's extra spooky. Add to this the owl's taste for decaying flesh, and the almost universal acceptance of the owl as a symbol of death becomes totally understandable.

Interview with an Owl

Nicknames: "Night Hag," "Corpse Bride"

Distinguishing feature: Huge, saucer-like eyes—no eyeliner needed here

Occupation: Harbinger of death—you really don't want to see or hear this dude, but in case you do, be sure to keep your pockets turned out. Owls are totally uninterested in unfashionable souls!

Friends: A bit of a loner, though occasionally flies about at night with a witch

Odd couple: This very dumb bird is best buds with that really smart Greek goddess Athena. Go figure!

Talent: "I can look behind me, beside me, in front of me, all around me. You can't escape my notice. I see everything, everyone. Be afraid; be very afraid."

Fashion sense: Prefers the pale, ghostly look

Table manners: None. Doesn't chew its food and is constantly vomiting up bones and feathers and fur—definitely *not* someone you would bring home for dinner.

Thing most dislikes about self: "Too small. Come on, the harbinger of death should be a big, scary dude. Maybe if I fluff up my feathers a bit more…"

Favorite saying: "I don't give a hoot!"

Favorite haunt: Graveyards—loves the smell of rotting flesh! Who doesn't?

SCARY SPIDERS

Attacks of the Arachnids

Spiders, those many-legged little creatures that scurry around and make many people shiver with fear, are a popular Halloween decoration. With their webs stretched all over indoors and out, spiders remind us of haunted houses and symbolize darkness.

Creepy Crawlies

Do you like movies? Do you like to be scared? Why not watch one of these scary spider flicks next Halloween?

 Tarantula **(1955).** Some scientists in Congo have developed a growth serum that they test on themselves and a tarantula. The result? The scientists die and the tarantula escapes from its cage to wreak havoc on the surrounding area, killing and eating people and cattle.

Horrors of Spider Island **(1967).** A group of women from New York City are being flown to Thailand by a nightclub owner named Gary. The plane crashes over the ocean and the group ends up on a deserted island. Gary is attacked by a large spider and turned into a human-spider. He attacks the women until he is finally killed.

Tarantulas: The Deadly Cargo **(1977).** A plane carrying South American coffee beans crashes over a Californian town after the pilot is killed by stowaway tarantulas. The spiders create havoc in the community, killing several people, before they are finally destroyed themselves.

Arachnophobia **(1990).** A deadly, newly discovered spider from Venezuela hitches a ride to a California town on the body of a scientist it has just killed. There, the spider mates with a local spider, creating a large family of killer spiders that terrorize the community. The movie stars Jeff Daniels and John Goodman.

Eight-legged Freaks **(2002).** Little spiders become monstrous beasts after a chemical spill causes them to mutate. These big, bloodthirsty beasts terrorize the local populace, who must band together against them. The cast includes David Arquette and Scarlett Johansson.

DID YOU KNOW?

Arachnophobia, or fear of spiders, is the most common phobia suffered by people.

Miss Muffet's Medieval Medicines

Imagine if instead of having to take a daily vitamin pill, your parents insisted that you swallow a spider! That is exactly what the daughter of the 16th-century doctor Thomas Mouffet was forced to do. Her learned father firmly believed in the healing powers of these leggy beasts and wished for his daughter to benefit from them. His daughter's unusual daily "vitamin"—possibly eaten along with a bowl of curds and whey—is the source of the well-known nursery rhyme!

Dr. Mouffet was not the only early healer who used spiders as part of his pharmaceutical supplies. In the Middle Ages, live spiders were coated in butter and swallowed to stop an asthma attack, and their webs were a common remedy for warts. Conversely, in the 10th century, snails were crushed and fried and then smeared on spider bites. Powder made from crushed spiders was popularly believed to cure sexual impotence during the medieval and Renaissance periods. Their webs were effective as bandages to staunch bleeding.

These types of remedies could still be found in the 19th century. A remedy for jaundice used in Wessex was to eat a live spider wrapped in its own web. In Kentucky, spiders were eaten in handfuls on bread and butter for the relief of constipation.

Interestingly, about a century ago, scientists discovered that a fever-reducing drug called "arachnidin" could be produced from spider webs.

DID YOU  KNOW?

In Cambodia, a certain species of tarantula is fried and eaten as a snack.

A Web of Knowledge: Spooky Spiders

* There are approximately 73,000 types of spiders in the world.

* The world's largest spider is the South American Goliath bird-eating tarantula. It has a leg span of up to 12 inches.

* The world's five deadliest spiders are (1) Sydney funnel-web of Australia; (2) black widow of Africa; (3) redback of Australia; (4) banana spider of South and Central America; and (5) brown recluse of North America.

* Spiders inject their victims with paralyzing venom, then they vomit up acidic digestive juices all over the immobile but still living victim. This substance dissolves the victim's body to mush so that the spider can eat it.

* A spiders' legs end in two or three claws, each of which can pivot back and forth.

* Almost all spiders have eight simple eyes. Their placement on the head varies among species.

* Spider webs are five times stronger than steel of the same size.

* Throughout their lifetime, each person swallows approximately eight spiders while asleep.

* The Central and South American banana spider, so called because of its favorite haunt, produces enough venom to kill six adult humans.

DID YOU  KNOW?

In 1876, the Chinese gave England's Queen Victoria a silk gown made from thousands of spider webs!

The Spider King

King Louis XI (r. 1423–83) of France was nicknamed the "Spider King" because of the web of terror and control he wove using his network of spies. He also had a penchant for torturing and killing his enemies.

NEWSFLASH!

Babies Left Fatherless After Wife Kills Hubby

North America: Sources say that a single mother gave birth to 40 infants yesterday. The mother (whose name cannot be released, to protect her children) was recently widowed. She is reported to have killed her husband in a fit of passion following what must have been a very *unsatisfying* sexual encounter between the two. The woman, who is being referred to as the "Black Widow," remains unfazed at the immense task of raising such a large family on her own. She claims that she is not the first woman in her family to have done so. This reporter suggests that all men give this woman and her sisters a wide berth in the future.

Kiddie Cannibals

Australia: The remains of an Australian woman were found in her home earlier today by another woman, who was hired to come by once a week to clean the place. The dead woman had recently become the mother to a large brood of infants. A neighbor stated that the woman appeared to have been exhausted from the enormous work required to raise so many children. One child told police that his mother had collapsed. Hungry, the children had bitten her and drunk her blood. When there was no more blood left, they resorted to eating her body. Another child said that by vomiting on the body, the flesh became softer and easier to suck up. The country is appalled, and authorities are uncertain what should be done with the children. A memorial service for the mother is scheduled for later this week.

WEREWOLVES ON THE PROWL

Halloween is a time to scare and be scared. It is
a festival of the dead, and many of the creatures
commonly linked with the holiday are also closely connected
with death, the dead or the fear of dying. Werewolves,
vampires, zombies and Frankenstein are monsters found
everywhere across North America on October 31.
The werewolf is a mythical being with roots in the distant
past that has terrorized the imaginations of Europeans and
their North American descendants for centuries. Vampires
are the living dead, while zombies are the undead.
Frankenstein is a hideous being made from the body parts of
many dead people. This section explores some of the folklore
surrounding these supernatural monsters.

The Wolf Stone

In the Fichtel Mountains of Germany stands a large stone cross known locally as the Wolfstone. It reputedly marks the grave of an old woman/werewolf. Years ago, something, likely a wolf, was stealing sheep in the area. No one was able to catch the creature responsible until a local marksman was invited to help. However, he, too, was unable to kill the beast, though it was thought that he may have injured it. The next day, an old woman was seen limping. A shepherd accused her of being a werewolf, and the local authorities imprisoned her for questioning, but she somehow escaped. Later, she returned as a werewolf to the shepherd with his flock. She attacked him, but he managed to kill her with a silver-bladed knife. As the wolf lay dying, it transformed back into the old woman. The werewolf was buried 20 feet below ground, and a stone cross was placed on the spot.

Wolf Rock

Near the village of Eggenstedt, Germany, is a large rock. Locals call it the Werewolf Rock, stating that it marks the spot where a werewolf was killed. The werewolf had appeared to the villagers for years in the form of an old man. He would wander out of the Brandsleber Forest and offer to assist with tasks for payment. Many times he helped a shepherd named Melle watch his flock. Each time, the old man requested a particular spotted lamb as payment, and every time, Melle refused. Finally, the old man stole the sheep. The next time Melle encountered him, the old man taunted Melle. Angry, Melle raised his shepherd's crook to hit the old man, who suddenly turned into a wolf. Melle's dogs chased the wolf, cornering it. The old man took several shapes in an attempt to save his life, but failed. Werewolf Rock, where the dogs killed the werewolf, is said to still be haunted by an evil spirit.

Nineteenth-century Shape-shifters: A Prosperous Disguise

In Hungary, during the 1870s, there lived a Roma man named Kropan with his wife. They were very poor. One night, Kropan discovered his wife leaving the house at night. Curious, he waited up for his wife to return. Later, a wolf entered their hut carrying a dead sheep. Kropan fainted from fear. The next day, the couple had lamb to eat. And so things continued. There was even enough meat to sell some in a neighboring village. Eventually, Kropan and his wife were able to purchase an inn with the profits. The other villagers were becoming suspicious, however, at the couple's newfound wealth and the ample supply of meat on the inn's menu. They began to suspect that the couple was responsible for the recent thefts of farm animals. Kropan and his wife were seized, and the local priest attempted to exorcise them. When the holy water touched the woman's skin, it burned, and she screamed in pain before vanishing completely. Kropan was murdered by the angry mob. Two of the villagers spent six years in jail in Ilova for Kropan's death. They were released in 1881.

The French Sorcerer

In 1879, at Serisols in Sainte-Crois, there lived a miller named Bigot with his wife and their children. The miller was believed by locals to be a sorcerer. According to the children, their mother got up one morning and went outside to wash some laundry in the yard, leaving her husband asleep in bed. While scrubbing, she was surprised to see a large beast of some sort staring at her from across the yard. Frightened, the woman grabbed a piece of wood and threw it at the animal, hoping to scare it away. The wood hit the creature in the eye. The children stated that at that very moment, their father awoke, screaming, "Wretch, you have blinded me." For the rest of his life, the miller wore a patch over one eye.

The Were-coyote of Saskatchewan

In 1887, the mining families in southern Saskatchewan were terrorized by a vicious coyote. This large, red beast was responsible for the deaths of several people. One night, a young miner spotted the animal by the light of the full moon. Terrified, he nonetheless tracked it until he was able to get a good shot. He fired a gold bullet at it, wounding it. He attempted to follow the trail of blood but was unable to because of the falling snow. Two days later, a local Native reported that Red Morgan, an old miner, had been found dead in his cabin from a gunshot. Upon examining the body, it was discovered that Red Morgan had been shot with a gold bullet. No one was ever troubled by the were-coyote after that.

How to Tell if Your Friend Is Really a Werewolf

☐ My friend has a uni-brow.

☐ My friend is exceptionally hairy.

☐ My friend has hair on the palms of the hands.

☐ My friend is never around whenever there is a full moon.

☐ My friend's ring finger is longer than the middle finger.

☐ My friend has purple pee.

☐ My friend has small, pointy ears.

☐ My friend was born on Christmas Eve or Christmas Day.

☐ My friend's fingernails are more like claws than nails.

☐ My friend's parents are werewolves.

If you checked off all the boxes, your friend is suspiciously similar to a werewolf.

The Werewolf of Ansbach

It is 1685 and the small Bavarian town of Ansbach is in an uproar. Several women and children have been murdered in the past year. Also, numerous cattle have been killed. Rumor has it that the killings are the work of a large, vicious wolf possessed with the spirit of the recently deceased mayor. He had been a mean man, and his death had not been the cause of much mourning.

Finally, someone kills the wolf. The body of the wolf is dressed in the clothes of the former mayor. Its snout is cut off to allow for a mask of the mayor to cover its face; a wig is placed on the wolf's head. The stuffed body of the werewolf is displayed in the town square. The townspeople rejoice because they and their cattle are safe. Soon, the wolf in the mayor's clothing will be moved to the museum as proof werewolves really do exist.

DID YOU KNOW?

In 1988, the Fox Broadcasting Company set up a werewolf hotline and, within six weeks, had received 340,000 calls from people in the U.S. who claimed to have seen a werewolf or believed that a particular crime had been committed by one.

Rock-a-bye Werewolf

According to European folk traditions, some people are destined to be werewolves. Here are some of the folk beliefs surrounding those ordained for a life of transformations every full moon:

- Infants conceived during a new moon will become werewolves. (Sicilian)

- Sons of priests are fated to turn into werewolves on nights with a full moon. (French)

- Babies born on Christmas Day were cursed to take the form of a werewolf every year during the Octave of the Nativity. (Campanian)

- A baby whose pregnant mother crawled naked through the caul of a foal to avoid the pains of childbirth will become a werewolf. (Scandinavian)

- If a couple has six daughters in a row, one of them will be a werewolf. (German)

Dates to Remember

5th century BCE: Herodotus reports on a people called the Neuri, whom he claimed transformed into wolves once every year.

1198: Marie de France writes "Bisclavret," the first poem about a werewolf. In it, a rich baron is trapped in his wolf form by his treacherous wife.

1257: The use of torture as an interrogation technique when questioning suspected werewolves is officially sanctioned by the Church.

1407: The first recorded prosecution, conviction and execution of people as werewolves occurs in Basel, Switzerland.

1520–1630: French inquisitors recorded 30,000 cases of werewolves.

1999: The U.S. Patent and Trademark Office refuses to patent a technique to create a human-animal hybrid creature.

Werewolves in the Movies

Perhaps you would prefer to stay in this Halloween and enjoy a scary movie with a group of friends? Well, there is definitely no shortage of scary movies from which to choose. More than 220 movies alone have included a werewolf character! Here are some suggestions:

The Wolf Man (1941). The heir to a Welsh estate returns home from America only to be bitten by a gypsy werewolf. Soon, this new werewolf is wreaking havoc in the area.

I Was a Teenage Werewolf (1957). A troubled teen (Michael Landon) finds himself the subject of an experiment in regression therapy by his psychiatrist. The experiment goes horribly wrong, and the youth taps into his repressed werewolf.

The Curse of the Werewolf (1961). Leon is the illegitimate son of a serving woman and a beggar. Born on Christmas Day, Leon grows up to become a werewolf, terrorizing the small village in Spain where he lives.

The Howling (1981). A television reporter from Los Angeles goes on a retreat in northern California on the advice of his therapist. The place at which he stays ends up being home to a number of werewolves. Numerous sequels have been made.

An American Werewolf in London (1981). Two American university students travel to England. On their journey, they venture across some moors, where they are attacked by a werewolf. One boy is killed and the other is badly injured. While in hospital, the survivor is visited by the ghost of his companion, who warns him that he, too, will become a werewolf at the next full moon.

Silver Bullet **(1985).** A small town is gripped by fear as its residents are terrorized by a werewolf. Based on Stephen King's *Cycle of the Werewolf,* the movie tells the story of how the murderous citizen is finally identified.

Brotherhood of the Wolf **(2001).** This loosely historical movie is based upon the series of killings that took place in the 18th-century French countryside. The local people believed the horrible deaths were the work of a werewolf nicknamed "The Beast of Gevaudan."

Dog Soldiers **(2002).** Six British soldiers parachute into Scotland to participate in a training exercise—or so they think. In reality, they have been brought to the area to serve as bait to lure out a pack of vicious werewolves being hunted by another group of Special Forces soldiers.

VICIOUS VAMPIRES

Bram Stoker's *Dracula*

Count Dracula of Transylvania has purchased Carfax House in England. A young solicitor, Jonathon Harker, travels to Transylvania to close the deal. He is imprisoned in Dracula's castle, where he discovers that the count is a vampire. The count flees to England, where he attacks Lucy Westenra, a friend of Jonathon's fiancée, Mina Murray. Lucy becomes ill and eventually dies from severe blood loss. Professor Abraham Van Helsing, a former tutor to one of Lucy's suitors, suspects that the young woman was the victim of a vampire and has now become one herself. His suspicions are confirmed when she leaves her grave the night after her death. In the morning, Van Helsing, Lucy's fiancé and two former suitors drive a wooden stake through Lucy's heart to kill the vampire.

In the meantime, Jonathon has escaped from Dracula's castle and returned to England, where he warns the others. Dracula attacks Mina, but he is unable to complete her transformation because Van Helsing and the other men stop him. The men search for him in England and eventually track him back to Transylvania, where they kill him just before he reaches the safety of his castle.

DID YOU KNOW?

Bram Stoker was a sickly child who spent a lot of time in bed listening to his Scottish mother tell him stories about *glaistigs*, evil female fairies that drank blood obtained either by slashing the throats of hunters or sucking the veins of human lovers. Stoker was later inspired to write *Dracula* by a nightmare he had. With bedtime stories like these, is it any wonder the man had nightmares!

Vlad Tepes: The Original Count Dracula

The model for Bram Stoker's *Dracula* was a real man who lived and ruled in the 15th century. Who was he?

📖 Vlad Dracula III (1431–76) was a Wallachian count. Wallachia is an area of Romania just south of Transylvania.

- "Dracula" means "son of the Devil or dragon" in Romanian. Vlad's father was a member of a secret fraternity known as the Order of the Dragon, founded by King Sigismund of Hungary in 1410 and dedicated to keeping the Turks out of Europe. In recognition of his courageous efforts against the Turks, his father became known as "Vlad the Dragon."

- Vlad spent part of his youth as a hostage at the court of the Turkish sultan Murad II to ensure his father's faithful recognition of their joint treaty.

- After attaining power, Vlad "Tepes" ("the Impaler") sought revenge on the elite *boyars* (noblemen) who had murdered his father and his brother. He ambushed them and their families at a banquet at his castle—he impaled the older people on stakes, the younger ones he forced to construct a new castle under appalling conditions.

- Vlad the Impaler enjoyed picnicking in a forest of stakes in which his victims were impaled—some dead, others in agony. During his wars with the Turks, many Turkish soldiers found themselves impaled through the mouth, heart, stomach or anus with a wooden stake and left to die a horrendous death. (The original Dracula's preferred method of torture makes one wonder if there is a connection between Vlad the Impaler's habit of staking his victims and the idea that you can destroy a vampire by driving a wooden stake through its heart.)

- On April 2, 1459, he supped among the impaled bodies of thousands of captured Saxons in the Transylvanian town of Brasov.

- When the castle of Vlad Tepes was attacked by the Turks, he fled using a secret passage, leaving his wife to fend for herself. She threw herself off the castle walls to escape capture.

- Any women caught committing adultery were ordered by Vlad to be skinned alive.

Dracula the Hero?!

In Romania, Vlad Dracula III is revered as a hero of the people. His efforts and successes at keeping the Turks out of Romanian territory made him a hero of Romanian independence.

DID YOU KNOW?

The current holder of the title of Count Dracula is Ottomar Rudolphe Vlad Dracul Prince Kretzulesco. He is a Red Cross volunteer in Germany, where he organizes blood drives!

The Corpse and the Vampire

Most of the physical characteristics used in the past to identify a corpse as a vampire can now be explained as natural phenomena by forensic pathologists:

- *The body is bloated; the vampire moans when a stake is driven into it.* Bloating is the result of a buildup of gases produced by the decomposition of the internal organs. The "moan" is the sound of the gases escaping.

- *The corpse has bloody lips.* The gases produced by the decomposition of the internal organs press against the lungs, which are also deteriorating. This forces the blood and other bodily fluids from the lungs and out through the mouth.

- *The body is warm.* Decomposition produces heat.

- *The body is not in rigor mortis.* Rigor mortis is actually only a temporary condition after which the body regains its elasticity.

- *The hair and nails have continued to grow.* Actually, they only appear to grow because the skin shrinks back.

- *The corpse bleeds.* Blood coagulates after death. However, in cases where death was sudden and the oxygen supply abruptly cut off, the blood will become liquid again and remain so.

The Start of the Scare

A report by Johann Fluckinger, a Belgrade official, about a local man named Arnold Paole who had apparently turned into a vampire after his death set off the vampire scare in 18th-century Europe.

In 1727, Paole, a Serbian soldier who had spent time in Greece and the Levant, returned home to the village of Meduagna. He married Mina, the daughter of a neighboring farmer. His wife questioned him as to what was always troubling him. He told her that he had been visited by a vampire while stationed in Greece, and even though he had killed it, he still felt cursed. Paole died shortly after the couple's marriage, from wounds he received falling out of a hay wagon.

Villagers soon began dying mysteriously. Officials from Belgrade were summoned to exhume and examine Paole's corpse. They found that it had shifted in the grave. Its mouth was open and there was blood on the lips. The priest sprinkled holy water and garlic on the body, then officials drove a stake through the heart, eliciting a scream and much blood. The bodies of four other recently deceased villagers were also exhumed and their hearts impaled. All five were then cremated.

DID YOU  KNOW?

One reason that people say "Bless you!" after someone sneezes is to protect the person from vampires. It was once believed that the soul leaves your body momentarily during a sneeze, leaving you vulnerable for a vampire or some other evil spirit to enter your body and possess it. Saying "Bless you!" when someone sneezes protects that person from being possessed by an evil spirit, such as a vampire.

Bless You!

A Romanian folk tale tells the story of a young man who almost lost his soul to a sneaky vampire.

The young man is preparing to leave on a journey. He is in front of his house with his horse, almost ready to go. Nearby, a horse thief is awaiting his chance when he spies a vampire hiding in the bushes outside the window. The young man turns and goes back into the house. Soon, the thief and the vampire hear the young man sneeze. Before the vampire can seize the opportunity, the thief says, "Bless you!"—saving the young man's soul. The vampire is furious at being thwarted; he swells with anger until he literally bursts. The thief tells the young man and his parents about what almost happened. The family sees the remains of the vampire sprayed about in front of the house and are so grateful that they reward the thief with the horse the young man was to take on his journey.

NEWSFLASH!

Demetrious Myiciura (1905–73): Mr. Myiciura, a 25-year resident of Stoke-on-Trent, was discovered dead in his bed yesterday. Reports state that he succumbed to his lifelong fear of vampires. Neighbors claim that the man was a bit of an eccentric who avoided contact with other people. Apparently, he believed himself to be surrounded by vampires. (When questioned about this, locals were quick to assert their humanness, denying any involvement in the death of Mr. Myiciura.)

Since emigrating from Poland in 1948, Mr. Myiciura went to great lengths to protect himself from local vampires. Neighbors recalled that each evening, Mr. Myiciura was seen placing bowls of salt, garlic and urine outside every door and window of his house. Upon investigating the scene, police noticed large quantities of salt and pepper sprinkled throughout the house, as well as garlic cloves stuffed into every keyhole! The local coroner reported that his body was found with a bag of salt near the left side of his head and another between his legs. The cause of death was determined to be choking—apparently, Mr. Myiciura slept with a garlic clove in his mouth for additional protection! The garlic succeeded in keeping the undead from this unusual resident but was unable to keep Death itself at bay.

Vampires Be Gone!

Not too keen on the idea of the "undead" sucking out your blood? Here are some things you can do to prevent such an occurrence:

- Cook with garlic, wear stylish garlic clove jewelry and decorate your house with *trés chic* garlands of garlic.

- Need a nice beverage to go with your garlic-drenched meal? May I recommend a nice glass of water with a dash of vampire ashes?

- Crucifixes come in all sorts of neat shapes—minimalist, Celtic chic, modish Maltese and trendy Templar. Put one in every room.

- Blue is the new pink in the world of vampire-repellant clothing.

- Avoid visits to old mills—vampires love these places because they bring back memories of their golden years.

- Move to the tropics—vampires are prone to sunburns.

And, just in case…

- Keep a wooden stake in your purse (or in your treat bag).

Blood-red Riddles

Where does a vampire keep its money?
In a blood bank!

What do vampires cross the sea in?
Blood vessels.

What fruit do vampires like best?
Neck-tarines!

What type of dog does Dracula own?
A bloodhound.

Why doesn't Dracula have any friends?
Because he's a pain in the neck!

Who did Dracula ask to marry him?
His ghoul-friend.

Why did she refuse?
He had bat breath.

What do you get when you cross a vampire with a computer?
Love at first byte!

How do you say goodbye to Count Dracula?
So long, sucker!

Varieties of Vampires

Nearly every culture around the world has tales of vampire-like creatures that prey upon human beings, stealing their blood and life force. Their existence is not surprising because curiosity regarding what happens to a person's soul after death is universal—we fear the unknown and what the dead might do to those still living. Here is a list of some of these supernatural beings:

- **abchanah:** Bolivian vampire; lures victims in the guise of a kindly old man

- **algul:** Arabic female vampire that preys on the fresh corpses of children

- **bouda:** vampire of Ethiopia, Tanzania and Morocco that has the ability to transform into a were-hyena

- **brujas/brujos:** vampire witches of Mexican American tradition; sought out for folk remedies but also believed to transform into vampire bats

- **bruxsa:** Portuguese vampire witch that prefers the blood of babies

- **buo:** vampiric spirit of Borneo that inhabits the bodies of dead warriors

- **callicantzaros:** Greek vampire only active during the Christmas season (December 25 to January 7)

- **canchu:** vampire of pre-Columbian Peru that favored the blood of young warriors

- **chupacabra:** large, hairy humanoid bloodsucker with bat-like wings; usually attacks animals but occasionally people; majority of reports are from Puerto Rico, Central and South America, with some from the southern U.S. and Europe

- **dachnavar:** Armenian vampire that sucks blood from the toes of its victims

- **glaistig:** Scottish female vampire with the torso of a beautiful woman and the legs of a goat hidden under a long skirt; seduces men and then drinks their blood

- **kathakano:** Cretan vampire that blinds its victims with the razor-sharp, gleaming, white teeth in its always-grinning mouth

- **lilitu:** ancient Sumerian vampire that feasted on the blood of babies

- **lobishomen:** Brazilian vampire that preys on women, turning them into nymphomaniacs with its bite

- **loogaroo:** West Indies vampire; an old woman whose pact with the Devil requires her to supply him with blood; she can shape-shift into a glowing light

- **mullo:** Roma male vampire; 40 days after burial, it becomes active for three to five years; sexually insatiable—may cause the death of its human lover from pure exhaustion; can procreate with its widow

- **tlahuelpuchi:** Aztec vampire that preys on children and shape-shifts into various animal forms, but usually that of a turkey

- **yoruga:** bad-smelling Prussian vampire whose awful odor can be detected up to a mile away

NEWSFLASH!

Germany (1974): German police announced the arrest of a local man for vampirism yesterday. The man, known to neighbors as Count Lorca, was roused from sleep in his coffin after another man, a homeless drunk, complained that the count had bitten him in the neck and tried to suck his blood! The man claims to have been so frightened that he fainted on the spot. (The owner of a nearby tavern stated that the man is a regular who "faints" on sidewalks and in alleyways most nights.)

Neighbors of Count Lorca report that he was definitely eccentric. "Never saw him during the day," stated a woman who lives across the street. "Only ever came out of his house at night. A bit odd, don't you think?" Another neighbor remembered inviting the count over for a barbecue just after he moved into the area. "He thanked me for the invitation but said that he was allergic to sunlight. He also said that he preferred to eat his meat raw. After that, I just kept my distance."

The man who claims to have been attacked by Lorca said that the two met on a sidewalk a few blocks away. The count, seeing the man sitting alone against a run-down building, invited him over for a meal, offering him a place to sleep for the night. "You can imagine my surprise when I discovered that I was the intended meal!" the man exclaimed.

Count Lorca faces charges of aggravated assault and attempted murder. His trial will be held at a later date.

Little Vamplings

Just as some people are destined to be werewolves, others are fated to be vampires. There are many European folk traditions that state which babies will grow up to be vampires:

- Babies born with teeth. (Polish)

- Illegitimate infants born of two illegitimate parents. (Romanian)

- Babies born from incest. (Croatian and Serbian)

- A baby whose mother did not eat salt during her pregnancy. (Romanian)

- A baby whose mother was naked in the light of a full moon. (Breton)

- A baby who has six older siblings of the same gender. (Romanian)

- Babies born on Christmas Day—as a punishment for having been conceived by their mothers on the same day the Virgin Mary conceived Jesus. (Greek)

DID YOU  KNOW?

According to the Roma, a child born to a widow and her late-husband-turned-vampire has the ability to detect and kill vampires. Such a child is known as a *dhampir*.

NEWSFLASH!

May 2005: A Romanian court sentenced six men—
Gheorghe Marinescu, Mitrica Mircea, Popa Stelica,
Constantin Florea, Ionescu Ion and Pascu Opres—to
six months in jail for unlawfully exhuming a body. In
July 2004, the men, all relatives, dug up the corpse of
Petre Toma, a former schoolteacher. The men believed
Toma was a vampire that had been plaguing their
family. At midnight, the men ritually killed the vampire by driving a pitchfork into his chest, removing his
heart and sprinkling the corpse with garlic. They carried
the heart on the pitchfork to a crossroads, where
Marinescu's wife, son and daughter-in-law waited by
a fire. The heart was burned and the ashes mixed with
water. The family members then drank the mixture to
protect the rest of the community from the vampire.
The men claimed that this ritual for disposing of
a vampire has been passed down through their family
for generations.

ZOMBIES

Creating a Zombie

After years of research, ethnobiologist Wade Davis, author of *The Serpent and the Rainbow* (1985), came to the conclusion that zombies do exist; however, they are not dead people brought back to life, but living people who have been poisoned so as to appear dead and later revived.

A poisonous concoction is made from a number of noxious plants and animals, including the venom of bouga toads and sea snakes, ground millipedes and tarantulas, white tree toads, puffer fish, dieffenbachia plants and cashew leaves. The mixture must be carefully and precisely prepared or the results really will be fatal. The victim of the *bokor* (voodoo sorcerer) suffers terribly, experiencing dizziness, nausea, diarrhea and paralysis, among other things. Then, the victim is buried—alive. A day or two after burial, the bokor returns to the grave of his victim to dig the body out and administer another concoction, this one of zombie's cucumbers, sweet potatoes and cane sugar.

The zombie is now the slave of the bokor. Zombies are put to work doing everything from laboring in fields to cleaning houses. They are docile and inexpensive. They do not require much food. A zombie should never be given salt to eat—this will cause it to realize that it is not in its grave, and it will panic and go berserk.

Preventing Loved Ones from Becoming Zombies

In Haiti, relatives of the deceased will stab the corpse through the heart to ensure their loved one is truly dead and not the victim of a bokor. Corpses are often buried face down so that they are unable to answer the summons of an evil sorcerer. Some are even buried with a weapon to defend themselves. In Haiti, it is considered better to be dead than to become a zombie.

Real-life Zombies!

Records of allegedly real-life zombies exist. These are people who were believed to be dead and buried but who later returned to their loved ones. The two best-documented accounts appear below.

Felicia Felix-Mentor

Felicia Felix-Mentor was a Haitian woman who had apparently died in 1907 and was buried by her family. In October 1936, a haggard-looking woman resembling Felicia was found wandering in the area of her old childhood home, muttering to herself about how she had once lived there. The woman was taken to a hospital, where she was later seen and photographed by the American folklorist and ethnographer Zora Neale Hurston. The woman with the blank stare remained in the hospital, her former husband and brother vouching for her identity.

Claircius Narcisse

In 1962, Claircius Narcisse was declared dead at the Albert Schweitzer Hospital in Haiti and was buried by his family. In 1980, he returned home. He claimed that his brother, along with some other men, had drugged him to make him appear to be dead. Later, they revived him but fed him more drugs so that he only functioned in a zombie-like state, and they forced him to do their bidding. Claircius escaped two years later and remained in hiding until the death of his brother 16 years later.

DID YOU  KNOW?

According to the *Guinness Book of Records*, the largest gathering of "zombies" occurred in Ledbury, Hertfordshire, on August 6, 2009, with 4026 participants.

FREAKY FRANKENSTEIN

Mary Shelley's *Frankenstein*

In Shelley's book set in Switzerland, Dr. Viktor Frankenstein tries to create life using the body parts of dead people. He succeeds in bringing his creation to life but can't stand its appearance and leaves. The creature frightens everybody who sees it, making it hate itself and its maker. Rejected by everyone, it becomes angry and starts killing people in revenge, including several members of its creator's family. Dr. Frankenstein pursues his creation to the Arctic, hoping to kill it, but instead it dies from exhaustion. Dr. Frankenstein then kills himself.

Frankenstein Festival

Since 1972, a Frankenstein Festival has been held at Castle Frankenstein near Darmstadt, Germany, during the last three weekends of October. It is the largest Halloween celebration in that country.

Bits and Pieces

☠ Mary Shelley wrote *Frankenstein* for a friendly, scary story writing competition in 1818. She won!

☠ Frankenstein's monster in the novel is very intelligent, but in the movies, the monster is very dumb.

☠ Johann Konrad Dippel, a former resident of Castle Frankenstein, was something of a scientist and a magician. Stories about him state that he discovered how to create life and experimented with creatures made from human body parts. It is likely that these tales provided some of the inspiration for Mary Shelley's masterpiece.

☠ The mother of Mary Shelley was the philosopher and early feminist Mary Wollstonecraft. Shelley's father was the political philosopher William Godwin.

☠ The Romantic poet and philosopher Percy Bysshe Shelley was Mary Shelley's husband.

☠ From the time of her famous husband's death in 1822 until her own demise in 1851, Mary Shelley kept his charred heart on her desk!

GHOULS

Who Ghouls There?

People often hear the word "ghoul" in relation to Halloween, but few really know exactly what one is, except that it is some type of gross, dead thing. Well, for those who want to know, here are ghouls in a nutshell:

- A ghoul is a demonic being of Arabic folklore.
- Ghouls haunt cemeteries, caves and other dark, lonely places.
- They eat children, travelers and fresh corpses.

- Ghouls live underground and come out only at night.

- They are extremely strong and possess supernatural powers.

- Ghouls resemble filthy, pale humans and have red eyes, long, sharp teeth and long fingers with long nails.

- Ghouls sometimes appear in cloaks or shrouds but they are often naked.

- They can shape-shift into beautiful women to lure unsuspecting male travelers to their deaths.

- Hungry ghouls will sometimes reach up from the ground and grab a person's ankle to try to drag the individual down to his or her death.

- Ghouls have been reputed to spread disease and plague by means of winds and storms.

- They can disappear in a puff of smoke.

- Ghouls can transform into various animals, their favorite being the vulture.

- Ghouls can control the thoughts of those nearby.

- If you hit a ghoul really hard, you can kill it. However, be careful, because if you hit it a second time, it will come back to life!

DID YOU KNOW?

In 19th-century England, the term "ghoul" was applied to grave robbers who stole corpses and sold the bodies to medical schools.

GHOSTS, SPIRITS AND SPECTERS

A Green Ghost!

Some ghosts seem to be especially partial to Halloween festivities, making their annual appearance on that particular night alone. The Green Lady of Newton Castle in Perthshire, Scotland, is one such apparition. Her visits are said to be accompanied by her gravestone turning around in a circle three times.

Ghost of Halloween

At Minsden Chapel near Hitchin in Hertfordshire, England, the specter of a phantom monk is announced by the tolling of long-gone church bells at midnight on Halloween. As he slowly floats up a flight of stairs that was once in the chapel's northeast corner, strains of ancient church music can be heard.

Halloween Huntsmen

Specter huntsmen are known from all over the English countryside. At West Coker in Somerset, the sound of the hunters' hounds chasing their prey can be heard every Halloween. Some people even claim to have seen between 20 and 30 dogs running across the fields.

The spirit of another huntsman is said to appear each year near Bernshaw Tower in Lancashire. This hunter is said to be the ghost of Lord William of Hapton Tower, once the husband of Lady Sybil of Bernshaw Tower—a noblewoman who sold her soul to the Devil in exchange for supernatural powers. Unable to capture the heart of the woman he wished to marry, Lord William sought the advice of a local witch, who advised him to capture Lady Sybil when she shape-shifted into a white doe on Halloween. This he did with the aid of some hounds, including one that was really the witch in disguise. Despite eventually becoming the wife of Lord William, Lady Sybil continued to practice black magic. In the guise of a cat, she lost her paw/hand to a miller, dying soon after. Her ghost still haunts Bernshaw Tower while that of her husband, a hound and a white doe visit the tower every All Hallows' Eve.

Some spirits are much more elusive, having been sighted on just a single occasion. Such a shade is the unidentified ghost seen pacing the parapets of Dudley Castle in England's West

Midlands by a group of ghost hunters spending the night there one Halloween.

Another even more mysterious phantom disturbed the slumbers of guests staying at Blackness Castle in Stirlingshire, Scotland, on Halloween night. They were awakened to the sound of furniture being moved about in the room below theirs, but upon investigating, found that nothing had been moved. After returning to bed, the ghostly sounds could again be heard.

The haunting peal of bells heard off the coast from the ruins of Whitby Abbey in North Yorkshire are said to made by the bells lost at sea when the ship carrying them to London following the abbey's dissolution in the 16th century sank. These haunting sounds are not unique to Halloween but may be heard at any time throughout the year. However, if a couple is fortunate enough to hear them on Halloween, it is a sign of a happy future together.

Ghostly Giggles

What type of music do ghosts like best?
Soul music.

What is a baby ghost's favorite game?
Peek-a-BOO!

What do little ghosts drink?
Evaporated milk.

What do ghosts eat for dessert?
Boo-berry pie.

Where do little ghosts spend their days?
At a day-scare center!

What type of mistakes do ghosts make?
Boo-boos!

What is a ghost's favorite bird?
A scare-crow.

What do you say when you meet a ghost?
"How do you boo?"

Where do ghosts like to go on vacation?
The Dead Sea.

What is a ghost's favorite type of road?
A dead-end street.

Who do ghosts call in an emergency?
The Ghost Guard.

What do you call the ghost of a door-to-door salesman?
A dead ringer.

Ghostly Films

Want to see if you can spook yourself this Halloween? How about watching one of these "ghostly" movies?

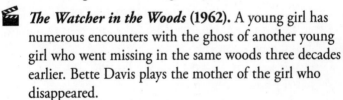

The Watcher in the Woods **(1962).** A young girl has numerous encounters with the ghost of another young girl who went missing in the same woods three decades earlier. Bette Davis plays the mother of the girl who disappeared.

The Haunting of Julia **(1976).** Following her daughter's accidental death, the despondent Julia (Mia Farrow) moves into a different house. Unfortunately for her, the house is already occupied by the diabolical ghost of another young girl.

The Shining **(1980).** The movie is based on the 1977 novel by American horror author Stephen King. Jack Torrance (Jack Nicholson) and his wife (Shelley Duvall), along with their son, Danny, move to the Colorado mountains, where the couple look after a hotel for the winter. Danny's psychic abilities alert him to the hotel's sinister past as well as to future events. When his writer father goes insane (after being tormented by the hotel's ghosts) and attacks his family, only Danny's ability can save them.

Ghost (1990). Molly (Demi Moore) and Sam (Patrick Swayze) are a couple very much in love. After Sam is killed by a robber, his ghost remains on earth determined to protect the woman he loves. Unable to communicate with Molly directly, Sam seeks the aid of a psychic named Oda Mae Brown (Whoopi Goldberg).

Sixth Sense (1999). In this movie, a young boy is terrorized by the unusual ability he possesses—he can see ghosts. Spirits appear to him seeking help. Mel Gibson plays the role of one of the spirits.

The Others (2001). Following World War II, a widow named Grace (Nicole Kidman) and her two children are living in a remote house on the island of Jersey in the English Channel. They are soon joined in the house by a nanny, a gardener and a mute girl. A series of strange and scary events follows, leading Grace to fear that the house is haunted.

The Ring (2002). A journalist, played by Naomi Watts, sets out to investigate the recent death of her niece. She discovers that the death may be linked to a series of teenage deaths in the area—the common link being a video each teen viewed a week before dying. After watching the video, the journalist and her son receive a phone call advising them that they have only seven days left to live—and unravel the mystery.

***Saint Ange* (2004).** In 1958, a pregnant young woman named Anna is hired to clean an orphanage in the French Alps. Only one orphan named Judith remains there—a young woman with mental problems. Soon, Anna begins hearing the footsteps and voices of former residents. She discovers that Judith also hears these sounds. Together, they work to uncover the orphanage's secret past.

Would You Dare…

The ghosts of the dead have long been thought to be most restless on All Hallows' Eve. In some places, legend states that certain ghosts appear each year on that haunted evening. Young people dare each other to chance an encounter with a scary specter. Would you be brave enough to try any of these Halloween dares?

Bloody Barnes

Della Barnes was buried in the cemetery at Paducah, Kentucky, and a statue of a woman was erected on her grave. Barnes was murdered in 1800 and one of her hands had been chopped off. According to legend, blood oozed from the hand of the statue each year on Halloween. Local youths would dare each other to go to the cemetery that night and look at the bleeding hand; tradition held that those brave enough to do so would be cursed for life. The statue has long since disappeared, but Barnes' grave is still there.

Footprint on a Grave

Jonathan Buck was the founder of Bucksport, Maine. A local legend states that Buck, a Puritan judge, sentenced a woman to death for witchcraft. She is said to have cursed him before dying, saying that he too would soon die and that her footprint would appear on his gravestone to always remind people that he had murdered an innocent woman. No record of this trial exists, but the outline of a shoeprint can be seen on the tombstone. Local youths try to summon up the courage each year on Halloween to visit this grave.

Spirited Encounters

The Session House on the campus of Smith College in Northampton, Massachusetts, was built in 1700. It now serves as a girls' dormitory. The building is full of hidden passageways. Six people are said to have lost their lives in the passageways—two young children killed by their own mother, two college students and two lovers. Each Halloween, the young women residing in the dormitory are given the opportunity to explore the passageways for 20 minutes—in the dark!—to try to encounter these spirits. To successfully do so confers upon the discoverer a greatly increased social status.

Ringing Hell's Bells

Would you ring the church bells of St. Catherine's on All Hallows' Eve? St. Catherine's Anglican Church is located five miles west of Prince Albert's penitentiary in Saskatchewan, Canada. The church is reputedly haunted. If the church bells are rung a dozen times just before midnight on Halloween, the resident ghost will reputedly respond with an extra chime. This has led to the church gaining the surprising nickname "Hell's Bells"!

Do You Believe in Ghosts?

- In a 1971 study conducted in the United Kingdom, 50 percent of respondents claimed to have had contact with a dead spouse.

- Forty-two percent of Americans claim to have been in contact with someone who has died, according to a 1984 survey conducted by the University of Chicago.

- A poll conducted by Britain's Channel Four Television in 1987 revealed that 59 percent of English people believed some buildings to be haunted.

- Thirteen percent of the people who visited Florida's Epcot Center in Disneyworld in 1987 said that they had seen a ghost.

- A 1999 survey revealed that 42 percent of Britons believe that ghosts exist.

- In Norway, road signs mark the spots where ghosts have been spotted.

- Buried in New Orleans' oldest cemetery, St. Louis Number One, is Marie Laveau, the legendary 19th-century voodoo queen. Her tomb is frequently visited by fellow voodoo practitioners who draw red "X"s on it in an attempt to communicate with her spirit. Voodoo ceremonies are reputedly performed there at night.

Ghost as Witness

In Durham, England, in the early 17th century, a miller was visited by the bloody ghost of a woman named Anna Walker. She told him that she had been bludgeoned to death by one Mark Sharpe at the behest of her relative and employer, Mr. Walker. Having gotten the young woman pregnant, the landowner Mr. Walker decided to get rid of her for good. Anna told the miller that her body had been thrown into a coal pit. Skeptical at first, the miller eventually told local authorities about these strange visits. They investigated and, sure enough, they found Anna's body, the murder weapon and the murderer's bloody clothes all where her ghost had said they would be. Despite the lack of eyewitnesses, Walker and Sharpe were convicted by the courts on the strength of the testimony of their victim's ghost!

DID YOU KNOW?

In Iceland, the law allowed people who were being haunted by a bothersome spirit to prosecute the offending ghost in a court of law in order to obtain a restraining order against it!

No Ghosts Allowed!

Are you scared of ghosts? Don't want to see a strange apparition wafting your way on Halloween night or any other night of the year? Then perhaps you may want to invest in Ghost Away. This new product invented by Mary Elizabeth Feldman of Charleston, South Carolina, is a chamomile-based spray designed to eliminate ghosts in the same way that more common household sprays eliminate odors.

However, if you can't get your hands on a can of this, or you are old-fashioned, here is a list of traditional methods to protect yourself from spirits of all sorts.

- Turn your pockets inside out.
- Hold your thumb up.
- Plant lilies in your garden or keep a bouquet of lilies in your house.
- Wear a ring of basalt or chalcedony around your finger.
- Keep a pair of shoes by your bed, with one shoe toe pointing towards the bed and the other away.
- Hang a mirror in your front porch.
- Put salt on your doorstep.
- Keep a crust of bread in your pocket.
- Bury animal bones or an image of an animal and place the item in a sealed container by the doorway.
- Wear a match in your hair.

Hudson's Halloween Haunting

Willow Place Inn in Hudson, Quebec, is haunted by the ghost of a 19th-century serving girl named Mary. One day, during the uprisings of 1837, Mary overheard the plans of a group of rebels. She was discovered and murdered, and her body was buried in the dirt cellar of the inn. Every year since then, beginning on Halloween and continuing throughout November, her spirit perpetrates many poltergeist pranks, such as knocking over chairs and slamming doors.

DID YOU KNOW?

In the state of New York, it is the law that people selling a house believed to be haunted must inform the prospective buyers of its reputation.

FAIRIES

Beware the Pookas!

Don't let their small size fool you! These miniature men enjoy inflicting mischief and mayhem on their much taller neighbors—especially on Halloween. However, you probably won't catch a glimpse of these feisty fairies as they go about their annual trickery; they shape-shift into big, fearsome-looking black horses to carry out their dirty work. Keeping that in mind, you should probably avoid catching a ride on a black horse on Halloween—it might be a pooka in disguise! If it is a pooka, you are in for the ride of your life—and the end of your life!

The only person who has ever ridden a pooka all night and lived to tell the tale was Brian Boru, a legendary high king of Ireland. In the emerald isle, the folks of County Kildare and County Connaught have long refrained from sweeping their floors and tossing out liquid waste on the night they call "Pooky's Night"—they don't want to accidentally anger a passing pooka! These tiny terrors are said to wreak havoc on any crops that have not been harvested. They go from field to field spitting on any crops that have been left out and, in the process, poison them. Pookas also put a curse on all blackberries that have not yet been picked, rendering them unsafe to eat.

The pookas begin their reign at midnight on November 1. They maintain their dominant position until Beltane on May 1 when the good fairies take over to rule through the brighter days of spring, summer and fall. Pookas are most active at night, and, as with all fairies, their power increases when they are close to a spot that offers easy access to their

Otherworld home. So avoid fairy mounds on Halloween or you might be captured and hauled off to this other land.

DID YOU KNOW?

In Scotland, the Unsellie Court of evil fairies was said to prowl the countryside on All Hallows' Eve looking for people to make their servants.

It's Halloween: The Fairies Are Out and About

- At midnight on All Hallows' Eve, the dead and the fairies come to earth and celebrate: they dance to fairy music and drink wine till dawn.

- To free a mortal lover who has been captured by the fairies, one has to find the lover with his or her fairy captors on All Hallows' Eve and grasp that person unyieldingly no matter what.

- Fairies sometimes kidnap people on Halloween.

- Church bells were rung on Halloween to scare away the fairies.

- Witches and fairies fear iron and salt so some people used to put a bit of each on children's pillows to keep them safe on Halloween.

- It is dangerous to sit under a hawthorn tree on Halloween as it will anger the fairies who like to dance there.

- The Irish believe that you cannot refuse a request made by a fairy on Halloween.

- The Scots believe that fairies fight on Halloween.

- The Scots used to make an offering to the fairy folk each Halloween to protect themselves and their animals from the wee folk that night. A libation of milk known as *Leac na Gruagaich* ("Milk of the Hairy Ones") was poured on a special stone.

DID YOU KNOW?

Belief in fairies stretches from the present back into the shadows of history. A death registry from the 17th century lists three people who were literally frightened to death by fairies!

Do You Believe?

For centuries, people have believed in the existence of a variety of beings, such as fairies, elves, trolls, and goblins. The Irish poet and dramatist William Butler Yeats (1865–1939) claimed to have seen fairies, and the English poet and artist William Blake (1757–1827) said he had witnessed a fairy funeral. Sir Arthur Conan Doyle (1859–1930), creator of the ultra-rational detective Sherlock Holmes, also believed that fairies really did exist. Do you, too?

The Icelandic Tourist Board's official website stated that in 2004–05, approximately 80 percent of Icelanders believed in the existence of elves, and roads were often rerouted to avoid disturbing their traditional dwelling places.

DID YOU KNOW?

In Ireland, in 1959, the proposed route for a new road was altered when locals protested it would destroy a fairy palace.

The Changeling

In 1894, a murder revolving around a belief in fairies captured headlines across the world. In Clonmel in County

Tipperary, Ireland, a young woman named Bridget Cleary was tortured and burned to death because her husband Michael believed that she was a changeling (a fairy in disguise) left by the fairies who had spirited away his real wife.

In order to discover the true identity of his wife, Michael Cleary tortured Bridget with the help of her cousins, James, Patrick and Michael Kennedy; her father, Patrick Boland; her aunt, Mary Kennedy; and two neighbors, John Dunne and William Ahearne.

They forced her to drink a fairy "antidote" of herbs and milk, then held her over a fire. The latter was considered to be a sure way to expose a changeling because the fairies would come to its rescue, returning the real person as soon as its pain was evident. Afterwards, everyone except Michael Cleary was satisfied that this was indeed the real Bridget. The next night, Cleary subjected his wife to more torture, then he doused her with lamp oil, burning her alive.

Cleary was charged with murder as were the Kennedy brothers and their mother, Bridget's father, the two neighbors, another Kennedy cousin named William, and a herbalist named Dennis Ganey (who had prescribed the herbal "antidote"). All were found guilty of manslaughter. Cleary received a 20-year sentence of hard labor.

DID YOU KNOW?

In a lesser-known trial from 1843, a case of child abuse was dismissed in Penzance, England, when the parents convinced the court that the toddler was actually a changeling.

Protection Against the Wee Ones

Fairies may be small in stature, but they possess a great ability to create mischief and mayhem. There are several things you can do to protect yourself against such misfortune, especially when traveling in Ireland or going out on All Hallows' Eve:

- Turn your clothes inside out.
- Snap your fingers.
- Whistle.
- Ring a bell.
- Wear a cross or hang one in the room (one made from rowan twigs is especially good).
- Carry a horseshoe or hang one over the door (fairies are afraid of iron).
- Burn leather or bindweed.
- Carry a bouquet of daisies.
- Jump across a creek.
- Sprinkle around the milk of a cow that has eaten pearlwort.
- Hang a wreath of dried apples and heather on your door before sunset on Halloween.

If, despite your best efforts, you are cursed by a fairy on Halloween, here is what you should do to break the curse. Say the Lord's Prayer three times, pour salt on your table, rip one of your shirts, wash in a south-flowing stream or gather moss from a millstream.

DID YOU KNOW?

The word "fairy" comes from the French word *fey* meaning enchantment. "A fairy stroke" is another term for a seizure, while to be "touched by the fairies" means to go insane.

Spooky Words

- The word "ghost" comes from the Old English *gast*, meaning "life force," as in the expression "giving up the ghost."

- "Spook" is the Dutch word for "ghost."

- "Werewolf" comes from two Old English words: *wer* (man) and *wulf* (wolf).

- "Zombie" comes from *nzambi*, the Congolese word for "spirit."

- Transylvania means "land beyond the forest" in Latin.

- The word "monster" was once used to describe any deformed person, animal or plant. It comes from the Latin verb *monere*, "to warn," since such deformities were seen by Christians as warnings of impending danger and the need to reform one's behavior.

- "Warlock" (as male witches were called in Scotland) comes from the Old English word *waerloga*, meaning "enemy, traitor or devil."

YOU'RE THE APPLE OF MY EYE!

Falling at the end of fall, Halloween has always been in part a harvest festival. People celebrated and gave thanks for abundant crops. Feasting occurred as the animals that people were unable to feed throughout the cold winter months were slaughtered, and the fruits of the fields and gardens were enjoyed. Nuts, apples and grain naturally came to play a role in the rituals, traditions and festivities of Halloween.

Fertility Enhancers

Apples have long been associated with love and fertility. Ancient Hebrew women believed that apples enhanced a person's fertility: when attempting to conceive, a woman would bathe in water mixed with sap from apple trees.

The Greeks believed that apples were the special fruit of Aphrodite, goddess of love and beauty, made for her by Dionysus, god of fertility and abundance. Another Greek myth tells how Gaia, the earth goddess, first made golden apples as a wedding gift for Zeus and Hera as a symbol of the anticipated fertility of their union.

The Trojan War

It was desire for a golden apple that eventually led to the long war between the Greeks and the Trojans. Eris, god of strife, stirred up trouble by casting a golden apple into the crowd of divine guests at the wedding feast of Thetis and Peleus. The apple was addressed "to the fairest." Three goddesses—Aphrodite, Hera and Athena—all claimed the apple. Zeus called upon the Trojan prince, Paris, to settle the dispute. Each of the goddesses attempted to win the prize through bribery, with Aphrodite finally succeeding: she gave Paris the love of the most beautiful woman in the world. Unfortunately, that woman—Helen of Troy—happened to be married, and when she ran off with her Trojan lover, her husband King Menelaus and his allies fought to win her back. Here, the apple, so closely connected with love, reminds us that relationships are not just all sunshine and romance.

The Romans and Pomona

For the ancient Romans, apples were the fruit of love. They were also a sign of fertility. As such, they were connected with the autumn harvest festival in honor of the goddess Pomona. (The French word for apple—*pomme*—comes from the name of this goddess.) Pomona was the Roman goddess of fruit. Once all the crops had been gathered, the Romans gave thanks for the bounty with offerings of apples and nuts to the goddess Pomona. The people celebrated the successful harvest with feasting and games, including many involving apples, which were designed to reveal one's future spouse.

These fortune-telling rituals were easily adopted by the native Celts of the British Isles. They, too, associated apples with fertility. The Celts conducted numerous divination rituals as the veil between this and the Otherworld was believed to be especially thin at the end of October.

Who Will My True Love Be?

Here are a number of Halloween games using apples that are supposed to reveal something about the identity of a person's future spouse.

- Bobbing for apples. This is a very old divination tradition dating back to the time of the ancient Romans. Each girl carves her initials into an apple and places it into

a tub of water. The boys take turns trying to grab an apple out of the tub using only their teeth. The girl whose initials are on the apple that a boy picks will become his sweetheart in the future.

- Twist the stem of an apple, saying a letter of the alphabet with each twist. The letter you are on when the stem breaks will be the first letter in the name of your future spouse.

- Hang an apple peel by the front door. The first man to enter through it will bear the same first initial as your future husband.

- Twirl an apple peel around your head three times. Then toss it over your left shoulder reciting, "By this paring let me discover, the initial letter of my true lover." It will land in the shape of the first initial of your future husband's name.

- Eat an apple and then comb your hair in front of a mirror at midnight. You should catch a glimpse of your future husband in the mirror. (In New Brunswick, an unsalted, hard-boiled egg was substituted for the apple.)

- Cut an apple into nine pieces. Eat eight pieces. Then, toss the last piece over your left shoulder, turning around quickly after doing so. You will catch a glimpse of your future husband.

- Place an apple seed on each eyelid, naming each seed for a lover. The one that stays in place the longest signifies the truer love.

- Put an Allan apple under your pillow. In the county of Cornwall in England, Halloween is referred to as Allan Day, named after Allan apples. Young women there place an Allan apple under their pillow that night; the man in their dreams will be their future husband.

Snap Apple Night

In some areas of England and Wales, Halloween is known as Snap Apple Night. In the Swansea region of Wales, it is referred to as Apple and Candle Night. Both names come from the popular holiday festivity that involves catching an apple dangling from a string with one's mouth.

In some versions of the game, an apple and a lit candle are tied to opposite ends of a stick that is hung from the ceiling. The stick is then spun around. Players try to bite the apple and snatch it off the stick without getting burned by the candle. The first person to do so is the winner.

Another version of the game features numerous apples hung from different strings. The first young man to take a bite from one of these apples without using his hands will be the first to marry.

In a third version of snap apple, a girl embeds a coin into an apple hanging from a string. Two boys compete to grab the coin out of the apple first, without using their hands. It is thought that the boy who gets the coin will someday get the girl who placed it there.

DID YOU  KNOW?

"Snotching Night" is a Welsh name for Halloween that comes from "snatching the apple."

More Halloween Apple Lore

- Burying an apple in your garden beneath the rays of the moon on the night of Halloween nourishes the souls of the dead who roam that night.

- An apple buried in the ground on October 31 is said to attract unicorns.

- To ensure that the upcoming year is filled with good luck, eat a slice from three different apples on Halloween.

- Eat an apple before going to bed on Halloween night to ensure good health during the upcoming year.

- In times gone by, farmers used to go out to their orchards on All Hallows' Eve to secretly and silently bury 13 leaves from a harvested apple tree. This act would ensure a good crop the following year.

- Place three apple seeds labeled "toil," "ease" and "travel" on a hot element. As the seeds heat, they will fly off one by one. The last seed remaining foretells your fortune.

HALLOWEEN DIVINATIONS

Nutcrack Night

These glowing nuts are emblems true
Of what in human life we view;
The ill-matched couple fret and fume,
And thus in strife themselves consume,
Or from each other wildly start
And with a noise forever part.
But see the happy, happy pair
Of genuine love and truth sincere;
With mutual fondness, while they burn
Still to each other kindly turn
And as the vital sparks decay,
Together gently sink away.
Till, life's fierce ordeal being past,
Their mingled ashes rest at last.

–"On Nuts Burning, Allhallows Eve," Charles Graydon (1801)

In some areas of northern England, Halloween is called Nutcrack Night because of the practice of roasting hazelnuts that night. This tradition is thought by some to date back to the days when the Romans ruled Britain and celebrated their harvest festival in honor of the goddess Pomona with the roasting of nuts. Whether this custom's roots reach this far into the past is uncertain, but it has definitely been around for quite some time. Documents from the church in Elgin,

Scotland, record the chastisement of an old man for selling nuts for the purpose of divination on Halloween in 1641.

At some point in the past, the practice of roasting nuts to eat became intertwined with the festive tradition of fortune-telling. People waiting for the nuts to cook sought clues to the future in the manner the nuts burned. A nut that burns bright means good luck and wealth for the person who placed it in the fire. Another widespread custom involves placing various nuts in the fire, each named for a different friend or lover. The ones that burn slow and steady represent one's true friends and lovers, while those that burn quick and crack indicate fickle relationships. The Welsh believe that if the flames jump about when the nuts are thrown into the fire, the coming year will be full of fun and excitement; however, if they do not, the year will be dull and boring.

There are other forms of divination associated with Nutcrack Night. These involve the act of gathering nuts, which, in times past, the English believed was done by the Devil himself. Nonetheless, this practice involves a young, unmarried woman walking around a walnut tree three times, calling upon her love to bring her some nuts. When she looks up into the branches of the tree, it is said she will see her true love gathering nuts for her.

DID YOU KNOW?

Celtic mythology tells of a hazelnut tree that grew beside the Well of Enchantment. On branches overhanging the well grew the magic Nuts of Knowledge. Each Samhain, the Salmon of Knowledge would wait with an open mouth to catch these nuts as they ripened and fell from the tree, thereby increasing its knowledge.

Dream of Me!

Turn your boots towards the street,
Leave your garters on your feet,
Put your stockings on your head,
You'll dream of the one you're going to wed.

–Anonymous

It seems that nearly every locale throughout the British Isles has its own superstition regarding dreams and fortune-telling on the night of All Hallows' Eve. Most of the traditions involve placing a specific item under one's pillow in order to produce dreams of one's future husband. For example, at St. Ives in Cornwall, young women placed Allan apples under their pillows, while in Derbyshire, a sprig of rosemary or a crooked sixpence were preferred. Other items used by girls in England included bay leaves, yarrow or a twig of yew from the local churchyard. In Scotland, unmarried women slept with three stalks of oats under their pillows in the hopes of dreaming that their future husband was reaping the oats.

Colonists carried these traditions with them to their new homes. One Pennsylvania custom was a bit more elaborate than most. In it, the young woman had to walk out the front door of the house backwards and pick three blades of grass. The grass was then wrapped in orange paper and placed beneath her pillow to ensure that her dreams that night came true.

Not all dream divinations involved placing something under your pillow; sometimes a specific item was put near the bed. For example, in one custom, a glass of water with a small bit of wood in it was set by the bed: it was believed to entice dreams of falling off a bridge and being rescued by your future spouse.

Feeding the Future

A final type of Halloween dream divination centered upon eating a specific food before going to sleep. Some people thought that if they ate a dry piece of bread slowly and quietly while making a wish on Halloween, and then had pleasant dreams, their wish would come true.

A practice carried out by many a maid in Ireland and Scotland in order to discover the identity of her future husband was to eat a cake made of flour, salt and soot before going to sleep: in her dreams, her future husband would offer her a glass of water. In 19th-century Ireland, it was further felt that the young woman needed to both bake and eat this cake in silence if the process was to work. This gave rise to the term "dumb cakes."

Perhaps you would like to try out one of these traditions this Halloween? Who knows what your dreams might reveal about your future! Sweet dreams!

Pulling the Kale

In Scotland, there is a very old Halloween tradition known as "pulling the kale" ("kale" is another word for cabbage). On the eve of All Hallows, young men and women in Scotland are blindfolded and led into a garden. There, each person pulls a cabbage out of the ground. The condition of the cabbage is examined to foretell the future of the puller. For example, pulling a healthy cabbage means you are destined to go to heaven, whereas pulling a frost-bitten one foretells a future journey to Hell. The more dirt that clings to the roots of the cabbage, the greater the luck of the puller in the year to come. (Another version claims that if there is a lot of dirt clinging to the roots, the woman's future husband will be wealthy; if the roots are clean, he will be poor.) When the puller tastes the cabbage heart, a bitter flavor foretells a difficult life.

Most of the divinations connected to pulling the kale pertain to the identity of one's future spouse. When a young man pulls the cabbage and the stalk is straight, his future wife will be strong and healthy, but if it is crooked, she will be sickly. Furthermore, the shape of the stalk is supposed to resemble the figure of his future wife—tall or short, thin or plump. A woman placed her cabbage over the entrance to her house; the first man to enter would have the same name as her future husband. (In some areas, it was not the first man to enter—it was the first man upon whom the cabbage fell.) By tasting the cabbage, a woman could gauge the temperament (e.g., sweet, sour, bitter) of her future husband. Finally, pulling a cabbage with a white head meant that one's future spouse would be older than the puller, while a green head indicated a younger spouse.

Children in Scotland also used cabbages to determine the future. If a child wished for a new baby brother or sister, the child placed a cabbage on the doorstep.

Not all cabbages that were pulled up were used to divine the future, some were used for another favorite Halloween pastime—tricking! In the 19th century, boys took cabbage stalks and hollowed them out. The pith was replaced with hemp fibers that were set on fire. The boys then held up the burning stalks to the keyholes on people's doors and blew the flames through, frightening the occupants.

Born on Halloween

Were you born on October 31? Do you know someone who was? Babies born on Halloween are reputedly able to see and talk to ghosts. Those born with a caul (amniotic sac) on Samhain are believed to possess the ability to see the future. A number of famous people were born on Halloween:

> John Evelyn, diarist (1620)
>
> Johannes Vermeer, artist (1632)
>
> Pope Clement XIV (1705)
>
> John Keats, poet (1795)
>
> Alfred Nobel, philanthropist (1833)
>
> Dick Francis, author (1920)
>
> Dan Rather, newscaster (1931)
>
> Michael Landon, actor (1936)
>
> Jane Pauley, newscaster (1950)
>
> John Candy, actor (1950)
>
> Peter Jackson, producer (1961)
>
> Larry Mullins Jr., U2 drummer (1961)
>
> Dermot Mulroney, actor (1963)
>
> Robert Schneider, actor (1963)
>
> Vanilla Ice, rapper (1968)

A Bright Future?

Throughout most of history, fire has been people's sole source of light after the sun has set for the night. Not surprisingly then, many old Halloween divination customs involved candles. Some of them are listed below.

- 🎃 A single candle was lit and a person jumped over it. If it stayed lit, it indicated good fortune in the coming year, but if it went out, the coming year would be one of bad luck.

- 🎃 Twelve lit candles, one for each month of the year, were placed in a row. A woman jumped over them. The candles that went out signified the months in which she would marry; if none went out, she would remain unmarried.

One tall candle was lit and set on a table. Each woman walked three paces from the candle, then turned and tried three times to blow it out. The number of tries it took before the candle went out indicated her future marriage prospects: all still lit meant she would not marry; three tries and her future spouse would be a working man; two tries meant he'd be a man of rank; one try meant he'd be a rich man.

Halloween Divination Techniques: A Miscellany

According to *The Shepherd's Prognostication* (1729), to learn what the weather will be like in the coming winter, cut a wood chip from a beech tree on October 31. If the chip is wet, the coming winter will be bitterly cold. If it is dry, it will be a mild winter.

Throw a shoe over a house on Halloween. If it lands with the shoe toe facing the house, there is travel in your future. If it lands with the sole down, good luck is coming your way. If it lands upside-down, bad luck is in your future.

In Ireland and Scotland, a girl would throw a ball of yarn into an oven outside, keeping hold of one end. She would then slowly wind it back up until she felt resistance, as if someone (her future husband) were holding the other end. The name of her future husband would be magically transferred to her through the yarn.

Light a match over a sink and let it burn. If the burned tip falls off, the direction it points is the place where your future spouse will be found. If the match burns down without breaking, your future lover is already there with you.

Girls would sow hemp seeds on Halloween and then look over their left shoulder, hoping to catch a glimpse of their future husband.

- Walk around a chestnut tree three times. Then look up into the branches to see your future spouse's face revealed.

- A pioneer tradition was for a single woman to look into a spring or well by lantern light on Halloween to see the face of her future husband. The faces of any future children might also appear.

- In Herefordshire, on All Hallows' Eve in the early part of the 20th century, people would place an ivy leaf in a bowl of water overnight. In the morning, those people whose leaves were in the shape of a coffin would die in the coming year.

- On the Isle of Man, just before going to bed on Halloween, each person fills a thimble with salt and pours it into a pile on a plate. Any pile of salt that has settled by morning indicates that person will die within the year.

- Women used to melt lead and pour it into cold water. The resultant shape indicated their future husband's trade.

- Another old fortune-telling custom was called "scadding the peas." A piece of a bean was hidden inside a peapod. The peapods were cooked and then distributed to those present. The person who found the bean would be married within the year.

- An old American tradition was for a young woman to walk into her bedroom backwards at midnight on Halloween. She looked over her left shoulder while doing so and would see her future husband.

- Catch a snail on Halloween and keep it in a flat dish overnight. In the morning, the first initial of your future spouse's name will be written in its slimy trail.

Deathly Divinations

Just as there are numerous superstitious beliefs surrounding people who are born on October 31, so too are there ideas regarding people who die on Halloween. For example, in Ireland, it is thought that very ill or old people are more likely to pass away on this night than on any other night of the year. In Wales, people say that crows cawing around a house during the afternoon of the last day of October signals an imminent death in that household, of either a person or an animal. Another common superstition is that the ghosts of those who die on Halloween are unusually restless.

Both the Byzantine emperor John Palaeologus (1443) and the Indian Prime Minister Indira Gandhi (1984) died on October 31.

Halloween and Houdini

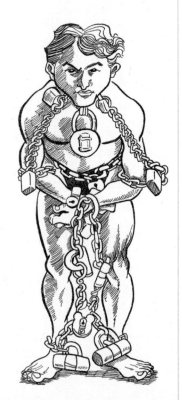

Probably the best-known Halloween death was that of the magician Harry Houdini in 1926. Houdini was fascinated with the idea of life after death and promised to contact his widow if his soul did in fact survive after he died. For years, his widow and many others held a séance every Halloween; whether Houdini contacted his widow is a subject fraught with controversy. Nevertheless, the anniversary of his death is still recognized by fellow magicians, and in the U.S., October 31 was declared National Magic Day.

PUMPKINS AND PUNKIES

The Legend of Jack-o-Lantern

Ever wondered where the term "jack-o-lantern" came from? Well, here's the old Irish story behind it.

One Halloween night, a disreputable Irishman named Jack became very drunk at the local tavern. The Devil, anticipating claiming Jack's soul later that night, joined him in the pub. Jack asked the Devil to share one final drink with him. The Devil agreed. Jack, however, did not have enough money. He asked the Devil to transform into some coins to pay for the drinks. As soon as the Devil did so, Jack dropped the coins into his wallet where he kept a small cross and locked it. The Devil could not get out. Jack bargained with the Devil, agreeing to release him if he left Jack alone for another year. The Devil agreed. Jack went merrily on his way and was soon up to the same old shenanigans.

The next Halloween, the Devil again came for Jack, and Jack again outwitted the Devil. Before he would follow the Devil to Hell, Jack asked the Devil to grab him an apple from a tree. The Devil agreed, but once he was up in the tree, Jack took a pocket knife and carved a cross into the tree trunk, trapping the Devil. The Devil was only able to come out of the tree after agreeing to leave Jack in peace for 10 more years.

So angered was the Devil by Jack's tricks that when Jack finally died a year later, the Devil refused him entrance to Hell. (God, of course, had denied him access to Heaven.) With nowhere else to go, Jack was condemned to wander the earth looking for a home, carrying a lantern to light his way.

In Ireland, people used to put out turnip lanterns on All Hallows' Eve. Some people claimed the lanterns were to scare Jack away. Other people said the lanterns were for Jack to replace his own, if needed—better to give Jack a lantern than to have him haunt you. It was widely known throughout the British Isles that you should never follow the light from Jack's lantern as he would lead you to your death in the swamps.

When millions of Irish people immigrated to North America during the Potato Famine of 1845, they brought their traditions with them. However, in the New World, they found a vegetable that was larger than a turnip or beet and easier to carve—the pumpkin.

Tasty Tidbits

- The world's largest jack-o-lantern was carved by Scott Cully on October 31, 2005, in Northern Cambria, Pennsylvania. The pumpkin was grown by Larry Checkon and weighed almost 1500 pounds!

- Scott Cummins of Perryton, Texas, creates intricate jack-o-lanterns. Lit from the inside with a light bulb, the varying densities of pumpkin flesh create fantastic illusions. Among the jack-o-lanterns he has carved are a baby in the womb, Winnie-the-Pooh, Gollum and Albert Einstein.

- It is believed unlucky by some to carve your jack-o-lantern with a black-handled knife.

- According to an old superstition, jack-o-lanterns carved from pumpkins planted on Good Friday offer the most protection against malicious spirits that roam about on Halloween.

- There were 10,540 lit jack-o-lanterns on display at the 1995 annual Harvest Festival in Keen, New Hampshire.

- 🎃 In the 2004 movie *Jack O'Lantern*, an evil spirit with the head of a jack-o-lantern avenges wrongs.

- 🎃 According to the *Guinness Book of Records*, Stephen Clarke carved 50 jack-o-lanterns in a single hour on October 31, 2008.

- 🎃 In Scotland, lanterns called "neeps" made from turnips, rather than pumpkins, are still preferred. Carved, they look eerily like skulls.

- 🎃 In the 1988 movie *Pumpkinhead*, some youths dirt-biking accidentally kill a boy. His father vows revenge and seeks the aid of an old witch who summons a demon called Pumpkinhead.

- 🎃 An early 20th-century musical was entitled *Jack O'Lantern*.

- 🎃 At the annual pumpkin-carving competitions held in Port Elgin, Ontario, underwater carving is one of the events. This environment makes the endeavor quite difficult: the air in the pumpkin causes it to float to the surface while the discarded bits attract hungry fish.

DID YOU KNOW?

The most people to get together and carve jack-o-lanterns at the same time is 965. According to the *Guinness Book of Records*, the record was set on October 31, 2005, by students in Scarborough, Ontario.

Punky Night

In Hinton St. George, Somerset, England, October 30 is known as Punky Night. A "punky" is a lantern made from a mangel-wurzel (a type of beet). Punky Night dates back to at least the 1840s. It is said to have originated when the men attending the annual Chiselborough Fair became so drunk that they could not find their way home and so their wives had to go collect them using a punky to light their way.

Today, on Punky Night, children go around with their punky lights collecting money. To carve a mangel-wurzel, cut off the top and scoop out the inside, leaving a thin layer of skin. The designs are carved into this thin layer but not through it—the candle will blow out if the skin is removed. The glow from the candle against the varying thicknesses of skin is orange. The town gives a prize for the best carved punky.

You Call *That* a Jack-o-Lantern!

- In 17th-century England, a jack-o-lantern was the name given to a night watchman.

- The eerie lights sometimes seen over the bogs and marshes in England and Ireland are often referred to as jack-o-lanterns.

- A common fall mushroom found east of the Rocky Mountains is named the jack-o-lantern. This poisonous, bright orange mushroom glows in the dark.

HALLOWEEN FOODS

Irish Treats

Ireland, the birthplace of the festival of Samhain, still cele-
brates the end of harvest and the coming of winter on the
night of October 31. The day is no longer called Samhain
but is known by a variety of names throughout the country.
In the northern part of the island, it is commonly referred to
as Halleve. In the counties of Wicklow and Mayo, a number
of names are used, including Vizor (or Vazard) Night, Juggy
Night and Blackman Night (the latter two come from the
tradition of painting one's face with burned cork). Hollantide,
Hugata Night (from revelers called "hugaidhes") and Bredeogs
Night (from the term for the wicker baskets and masks used
on this night) are also heard around the country.

No matter what October 31 is called, all across Ireland it is
celebrated with a feast comprised of several traditional dishes.
The best-known dish is probably colcannon. It is made from
mashed potatoes and turnips and sliced onions. In it are
baked four objects thought to predict the fortunes of the
recipients: a coin for wealth, a ring for marriage, a doll for
children and a thimble for spinsterhood. This dish is served
only on Halloween. Another potato dish that is served is boxty;
there are two versions: potato cakes and potato pancakes.

Stampy is an Irish Halloween sweet cake made by combin-
ing potatoes with flour, sugar, caraway seeds and cream.
Barmbrack, the Irish Halloween bread, contains raisins and
currants—possibly harkening back to the medieval custom
of passing out currant soul cakes on All Souls' Day. The porridge made from oatmeal husks that is eaten in Ireland on
Halloween may have roots that stretch back even farther
into the past: it is called *sowen* and is pronounced the same

as the ancient Celtic feast held at this time—Samhain (*sow-in*). This delicious meal is washed down with a drink known as lambswool, which is a concoction of apples, milk or ale, spices and sugar. Its name may have originated in the expression *la mas ubhal* meaning "day of the apple," a fruit highly valued and celebrated by both the ancient Celts and Romans.

Scotland

Across the waves in Scotland, another stronghold of the ancient Celts, the evening meal on Halloween also contains a number of special foods. The sowen porridge eaten in Ireland is also served here. The name of the Scottish Halloween dish *bonnach samhuinn* also recalls the old rites. It is made from corn meal with a custard topping. Another dish that recalls the old Celtic celebrations is bannock, a three-corned cake that is decorated with a design that looks like the rays of the sun. The coming of the long, dark and cold winter months provided the people of long ago with a special feeling of reverence for the warmth of the sun. In Lewis, during the Victorian period, the men and women ate these traditional dishes at separate tables.

DID YOU KNOW?

The people of western Brittany in France have also maintained their Celtic roots. They eat cakes called *kornigou* that are shaped like the antlers of a stag. The god of winter shed his antlers at the end of fall to prepare for his long stay in his kingdom in the Otherworld.

Baking Bannock with Bride

A pagan survival was evident in the early 19th-century Halloween bannock-making ritual at Rutherglen in

Scotland. A group of women would sit together inside a carefully marked circle to make the bread. The woman chosen to do the actual baking was called Bride. This is the name of the Celtic goddess of summer, whose yearly reign was nearing its end. The women seated directly on either side of Bride were referred to as Hodler and Todler. Todler would begin the process by taking a small piece of dough and kneading it before passing it around the circle clockwise; each woman in turn doing the same. Finally, when the dough reached Bride, she would bake it over the fire.

DID YOU  KNOW?

In England, women used to eat gingerbread men on Halloween, believing it would guarantee marrying in the future.

TRICK-OR-TRIVIA!

Trick-or-Treat!

In North America, the practice of children going from house to house begging for treats is a relatively recent addition to the plethora of Halloween activities. It was started by a few housewives as an attempt to bribe the neighborhood boys to not play any of their sometimes destructive pranks on the homeowners' property. It proved to be very successful. The practice slowly caught on in the 1920s but suffered a setback during the Depression years of the 1930s. During this decade, most people had no money to spare for treats, and many young people vented their frustration with the economy by pulling pranks on Halloween. However, following World War II, bribing youngsters with candy became the norm, and fewer and less-destructive tricks were played. Nevertheless, children still continued to carry noisemakers with them on their treating rounds well into the 1960s.

I Want Candy!

- Chocolate bars were invented in 1912; the first two types were Pearson's Nut Goodies and Goo-Goo Clusters.

- Before World War I, begging for treats occurred on Thanksgiving in the U.S. and not on Halloween.

- The 1920 packaging for the American-made Ze Jumbo Jelly Beans displayed the message "Stop Halloween Pranksters."

- The Disney film *Trick-or-Treat* popularized begging for candy in 1950s post-war America; it starred Donald Duck's three nephews Huey, Dewey and Louie.

- In the 1940s and 1950s, children were invited inside for homemade treats. This changed during the 1960s— children now remain out on the doorstep and are given store-bought candy.

- During the mid-1980s, there was a push in the U.S. for radiology units at hospitals to X-ray treats for razors and glass, among other things.

- In some places, trick-or-treating takes the form of "mumming" (performing for a reward).

- Ninety percent of parents admit to stealing Halloween candy from their kids.

- Fifteen percent of kids keep their Halloween candy for at least one year.

The Candy Man

Despite all the fear, only one death has ever been conclusively attributed to tainted Halloween treats, and that death was not a random act. In 1974, Ronald O'Bryan gave cyanide-poisoned sugar straws to his eight-year-old son, Kevin; his five-year-old daughter, Elizabeth; the two children of friends; and another child. Drowning in debt, O'Bryan decided to kill his children along with the others to try to make it look as though the act had been done by an anonymous monster.

Earlier, he had taken out a $20,000 life-insurance policy on each of his children, unbeknownst to his wife. Fortunately, only one of the children ate the candy before it was discovered to be poisoned. Unfortunately, that child—O'Bryan's son, Kevin—died. O'Bryan unsuccessfully tried to make it look like the children had received the candy from a stranger, but investigations revealed otherwise. Ten years later, O'Bryan was executed by lethal injection (the original date scheduled for the execution had been October 31, 1982).

DID YOU  KNOW?

In rural Saskatchewan, Canada, adults practice their own version of treating known as "trick-or-drink"! The costumed revelers are given a beer or other beverage so that they will not play any pranks on the house owners. It is all in good fun, and those participating go only to the homes of friends.

Trick-or-Treating for UNICEF

In 1950, some Sunday school children in Philadelphia collected $17 while trick-or-treating. They chose to give the money to the United Nations International Children's Emergency Fund (UNICEF). This was in keeping with an earlier practice in Canada whereby children collected money on Halloween for British children affected by bombing during World War II. The money was given to the Red Cross or the British War Victims' Fund.

The practice of collecting money for needy children around the world soon caught on across the U.S. and Canada.

Canada began to participate in 1955. Both countries have officially declared October 31 to be National UNICEF Day.

Today, children in Mexico, Ireland and Hong Kong participate as well. Children go door-to-door with little orange boxes collecting money for UNICEF and treats for themselves. Schools also set up boxes in the classrooms so students can make donations that way, too.

UNICEF was founded in 1946 after the end of World War II. Its mission is to provide health care and education as well as clean drinking water and food to the world's most disadvantaged children. To date, the Trick-or-Treating for UNICEF campaign has raised $41 billion. A few years ago, UNICEF also began to sell Halloween greeting cards at select Hallmark stores.

MISCHIEF NIGHT

A Time for Tricks

Before World War II, Halloween was mainly about playing tricks, with little distribution of treats. This was a time when youngsters, mainly boys, went throughout the neighborhood playing pranks to inconvenience their elders. Some of these tricks were relatively benign while others were fairly dangerous and did serious property damage.

The following is a list of pranks that were popular among the early settlers of Western Canada. Some of them are still being done by children today!

🦇 soaping windows

🦇 scattering dirt or flour on porches

🦇 egging houses

- putting toilet paper on fences and trees
- tying gates or doors shut
- removing gates
- disassembling carts and wagons and reassembling them on top of barns or haystacks
- tipping over outhouses
- hiding items in haystacks

Teenagers in rural areas still play pranks on their neighbors. Tricking has always been more common in rural areas where people know each other, and the whole community can enjoy (or condemn) the joke.

DID YOU KNOW?

In Scotland, playing pranks dates back at least to 1736 when some boys got in trouble with the kirk (church) at Canisbay for throwing cabbages at people's doors on Halloween.

Super-size Pranks

1934 Chicago World's Fair: When the Chicago World's Fair ended in 1934 on Halloween, 300,000 pranksters took control of 32 miles of streets, pillaging the booths and exhibits as well as drinking all they could get their hands on.

1945 Toronto Kew Beach Riots: During the Toronto Kew Beach Riots on Halloween in 1945, high school students and servicemen tore up fences and other wooden structures to light several bonfires in Queen Street East. Police officers were pelted with stones and concrete blocks when they tried to intervene.

Several "pranksters" were arrested. The remaining mob erected concrete barricades to keep out the firefighters. Then, nearly 7000 people marched to the police station to rescue those who had been arrested, turning on fire hydrants as they passed by. The crowd was finally dispersed by spraying them with water from fire trucks. The ringleaders spent several weeks in jail awaiting trial and received stiff fines.

 Tricking a Nation: *War of the Worlds* (by H.G. Wells) was broadcast by Orson Welles on his radio show on October 30, 1938. He did it as a newscast announcing an alien invasion of Grover Mills, New Jersey. Many listeners thought it was a real newscast. People panicked. Some fled. Some prepared to fight. It was a Halloween prank on a national scale.

DID YOU KNOW?

In 1939, more than 1000 windows were smashed by young hooligans on "Mischief Night" in Chicago.

Detroit's Devil's Night

Like most Mischief Nights, Detroit's Devil's Night occurs on October 30. Unfortunately, the mischief that took place in this city during the 1980s was of an especially malevolent variety. Arsonists were active across the city; 1984 had the most fires with 810. A lot of these fires and other forms of vandalism were the result of racial tensions within the city between the whites and blacks.

In 1994, Detroit mayor Dennis Archer began a citywide cleanup campaign to lessen the potential fuel for arsonists— vacant buildings were torn down and abandoned vehicles and garbage were cleaned up. In 1996, six southwest Detroit gangs entered into a Halloween truce to prevent arson. Today, the city has changed the name to Angel's Night in the hopes of further promoting good behavior.

DID YOU  **KNOW?**

The movie *The Crow* (1994) by director Alex Proyas was based on a comic book series by James O'Barr. It is the only major movie to focus on Detroit's Devil's Night. In it, a gang uses this night of mayhem to cover up their own illegal activities, such as extortion and murder. The gang kills two young people. The ghost of one of them is brought back by a crow the next year to exact revenge.

HALLOWEEN COSTUMES

The Roots of the Tradition

There are many theories as to how the practice of dressing up in costumes at Halloween came to be. Some speculate that the practice goes back as far as the ancient Celts, when Druidic priests and other members of the community are believed to have dressed in animal skins to lure away evil spirits. Another theory holds that the custom developed from the medieval tradition of dressing as angels and demons and parading around the parish church on All Saints' Day. Yet another suggestion is one that grew out of the early-modern Scottish practice known as "guising." This was when people dressed in frightening disguises and went out on Halloween to scare away any malicious spirits. However the practice of wearing costumes developed, there is no doubt that it is the best-loved part of the holiday for adults and children alike.

Popular Costumes of the Past Century

Halloween costumes have always reflected the society in which they were produced. A culture's most popular heroes and villains, as well as its economic situation, are seen in the Halloween costumes worn by the revelers. For example, during the 1920s, Charlie Chaplin look-alikes abounded. Topsys, Chinamen and Pierrots were also common, as were cowboys, Indians and hobos. The Great Depression saw children in costumes that were easy to piece together, requiring little if any money to create, such as hobos, robbers, Indians and pirates. These favorite choices were all considered outcasts in their society, and the costume selections reveal the prevailing atmosphere of economic hardship. Following the end of World War II, North American society entered a "fairytale phase" of perceived social perfection and bliss. This can be seen in the most popular costumes for young girls at the time—princesses, brides and angels.

The increasingly dominant effect of television on children and youth has been mirrored in costumes since the 1980s, not only in the characters chosen but in the preference for store-bought costumes over handmade ones (the latter sadly indicative of the general decrease in creativity brought about by being plugged into a machine for so many hours each week). In the 1980s, E.T., *Star Wars* characters, Ninja

Turtles, California Raisins, Freddy Krueger, and Jason from the *Friday the 13th* movies were all frequently seen at many doors on Halloween.

Since the 1990s, young girls have been apt to dress as their favorite Disney princess. For example, in 1994, with the release of *Beauty and the Beast*, Belle was a top choice. This trend of dressing up as current movie characters has continued into the 21st century, with *Harry Potter, Lord of the Rings, Gladiator* and numerous other superheroes being among the favorites.

Interesting Costume Tidbits

☠ The tradition of wearing a sheet as a ghost costume at Halloween comes from the medieval practice of burying people in winding sheets or shrouds.

☠ The first disposable paper Halloween costumes were sold by Dennison in 1916.

☠ In 1995, 80 percent of Halloween costume rentals were for adult costumes.

☠ Be careful what costume you choose for Halloween in Ireland. It may be illegal. You could find yourself spending the next year in prison!

☠ Need a Halloween mask? Joshua Taylor of West Jefferson, North Carolina, has more than 400 of them! Some of these masks were purchased. Some were made by the nine-year-old himself, using a rubber mask–making kit. Most of the masks are scary.

☠ Since 1998, an annual costume pageant for pug dogs has been held in Naples, Florida. The event is known as "Pug-o-ween." Since 2008, Seattle has also hosted one.

DID YOU KNOW?

In October 2009, the body of 75-year-old Mostafa Mahmoud Zayed sat decomposing on the balcony of his Los Angeles apartment for days. He had been shot in the eye. Neighbors did not report the dead body to the police because they had thought it was just a Halloween decoration!

Permanent Costumes

Some people are not content with dressing up just once a year. They want to be permanently transformed into something else. Such individuals resort to variety of methods in order to modify their bodies forever—plastic surgery, tattooing, implants, dental work.

Tom Leppard of Scotland is known as the "Leopard Man of Skye." His entire body is tattooed in the print of a leopard. He lives alone in a hut of sticks and stones on a remote part of the island.

Erik Sprague (a.k.a. "The Lizardman") wants to look like a lizard and has undergone extensive body modifications in order to accomplish this goal. He is covered in scale tattoos; his tongue has been surgically split and his teeth filed into sharp points. He even had a bony ridge implanted into his forehead.

Dennis Avner of California is completely covered in tiger-stripe tattoos. He has also undergone plastic surgery to elongate his ears, implant plastic whiskers and give him a cleft lip. He is nicknamed "Stalking Cat."

A Montreal man named Rick (a.k.a. "Zombie") is tattooed from head to toe with bones, internal organs and bugs. In short, in the space of only 24 hours, he turned himself into a living version of the undead.

SCARY HAUNTS

Haunted Harvests

Almost anywhere you go in North America in the weeks leading up to Halloween, you will see dozens of scarecrows decorating windows and yards. Long a harvest festival as well as a time to honor the dead, Halloween has numerous decorations that contain elements commemorating this harvest tradition—even in the largest cities.

- An annual children's Halloween event known as the "Scarecrow Festival" is held in Edmonton, Alberta.

- Since 1997, the town of Meaford, Ontario, has been crazy about scarecrows. So much so that each October, the town's residents dress scarecrows and pose them around the town for tourists—2043 in all in 2002! The harvest festival also includes a parade in which residents attired as scarecrows participate.

There are also several scarecrow festivals held in the U.S., including the Marshall Scarecrow Festival in Michigan, the Farmer City Scarecrow 'n' Pumpkin Festival in Illinois, and the Atlanta Botanical Garden Scarecrow Festival in Georgia. In Nashville, Tennessee, the Cheekwood Botanical Garden and Museum of Art has a scarecrow display each fall.

Throughout Canada's Prairie provinces, corn mazes can be found during the month of October. People of all ages go out to fields and attempt to find their way through the tall stalks. Once they have found their way out of the maze and emerge from among the corn, participants can often jump into the back of a horse-drawn wagon for a hayride.

Murderous Movies

Dark Night of the Scarecrow **(1981).** Four redneck men take the law into their own hands after a young girl is murdered. They kill a disabled man wearing a scarecrow costume, mistaking him for the girl's murderer. The man's ghost returns, complete with a scarecrow outfit, to take revenge on his killers.

Scarecrows **(1988).** Three evil scarecrows murder a man and his daughter along with the robbers who are holding the father and daughter hostage.

HAUNTED PLACES

Houses of Horror

Haunted houses are very popular on Halloween. These include
houses that are reputed to be haunted as well as those created
to give those brave enough to enter some spine-tingling moments.
Haunted houses (or Houses of Horror) that have been put
together for holiday fun can include a wide variety of decorations and scares. Spider webs and all sorts of creepy crawlies
stalk the halls. Vampires, zombies and other monsters lurk
around every corner waiting to jump out at the unsuspecting
guest. Chains clank and the wind howls. Sometimes, even

bowls of "brains" (cold spaghetti) and "eyeballs" (olives) are hidden behind a curtain so that visitors can reach in and feel them.

North Carolina's Spencer Mountain Volunteer Fire Department holds an annual Halloween haunted house fundraiser in a deserted old house on a hill overlooking the Catawba River. Interestingly, the building is reputed to be actually haunted by the ghost of a woman dressed in a white lace gown.

A movie theater in Tigard, Oregon, is another supposedly haunted place that serves annually as a haunted house. It was built in the 1970s and is now operated by Ray Latocki, as the 13th Door Haunted House. Latocki claims the theater actually has ghosts and they are good for business and help to scare the customers. There are five ghosts in all—a grumpy, old man dressed in black, a woman in her 30s, a man in his 20s, a young pioneer girl, and a cat.

In 1988, Trevor Kirkham, a Montreal professor, purchased a reputedly haunted house in Preston in northern England. Kirkham had planned to turn the 700-year-old house into a tourist attraction until he discovered that the house had no known ghosts connected to it. He had been duped. Kirkham sued the real estate agent, who had knowingly lied about the house being haunted. Kirkham won.

The Navaho were scared that the ghosts of the deceased would return to haunt their former homes. Thus, when a person died, not only was the body cremated, but their house was also burned to the ground

At the Movies

Terror in the Haunted House (1958). A young bride is horrified to discover that her new home is the house that has appeared in her nightmares for years. It was once the scene of several grisly murders as well.

 ***The Amityville Horror* (1979).** This movie is based on the strange happenings in the Long Island home of George and Kathy Lutz. This house was built on top of an ancient Indian burial site and was the site of a mass murder only a year or so before the Lutzes moved in. James Brolin and Margot Kidder play George and Kathy Lutz in the original 1979 movie. Ryan Reynolds and Melissa George star in these roles in the 2005 remake.

The World's Most Haunted Castle

Reputedly the world's most haunted castle, Glamis Castle near Forfar, Angus, Scotland, was once the childhood home of Lady Elizabeth Bowes-Lyon, the late mother of Queen Elizabeth II, and the birthplace of the late Princess Margaret. It is also the castle in which Macbeth murdered King Duncan, whose spirit is said to still roam the rooms.

- Janet Douglas, wife of John, 6th Lord of Glamis, and later the wife of Archibald Campbell of Skipness, was executed in 1537 on trumped-up charges of witchcraft brought against her by King James V as part of his vendetta against the Douglas clan. Her ghost is reputed to appear above the clock tower bathed in a reddish light.

- The ghostly apparition of a frightened young girl is sometimes seen gazing down from one of the castle's many barred windows. Legend states that her tongue was cut out to prevent her from revealing a family secret.

- There is a sealed, secret chamber in the castle's crypt said to be haunted by a former lord of Glamis, known as "Earl Beardie" (d. 1486). The earl is said to have lost his soul to the Devil in a card game. He can be heard cursing in the room where the fateful game was played.

🗠 The dungeon of Glamis Castle is said to be haunted by the ghosts of the many members of the Ogilvy clan who died there. The Douglas lord of the castle had offered refuge to the Ogilvy clan's warriors during a conflict between them and another clan. The men were taken to the dungeon where they were betrayed, being locked inside and left to die. Their bodies are said to have shown signs of cannibalism when removed.

🗠 In the late-Queen Mother's former sitting room at Glamis Castle is sometimes seen the ghost of a black serving boy playing hide-and-seek. The castle's chapel is haunted by a specter known as The Grey Lady. This spirit is often seen kneeling in silent prayer. The specter of a thin man, known as "Jack the Runner," can be seen sprinting up the castle's drive while the ghost of a madman glides along part of the roof at night. Another figure sometimes seen is a tall ghost wearing a long, dark cloak.

So if you like haunted houses and happen to be in Scotland someday, you should definitely take a visit to Forfar and see Glamis Castle and its ghosts for yourself!

Halloween with Howie

Every year, the staff of Government House in Regina, Saskatchewan, hosts many children at "Halloween with Howie." Howie is the name that has been given to the building's resident ghost. The children are given a short history of the building and taken on a tour, stopping to see the spots where Howie has made his presence known. Games, crafts and treats follow. The latter are combined in a craft called a "Howie Lolly" made from a lollipop and a tissue.

No one knows who Howie was in life, though the favored guess is Cheun, an immigrant from China who worked as the cook for Lieutenant-Governor Archibald Peter McNab. Cheun died there from pneumonia in the 1940s.

Government House served as the office and residence of the lieutenant-governor of the Northwest Territories and, later, Saskatchewan. Following World War II, the building was transformed into a veteran's hospital. Later, it housed the Community College, Art Board and Little Theatre. In 1984, it reverted back to being the office, though not the residence, of the province's lieutenant-governor.

Would Howie mind sharing his home if the lieutenant-governor decided to live there, as well? Probably not. Howie is a mischievous ghost, but not a dangerous one. His antics are harmless, such as moving items, opening and closing doors and walking about noisily, or sometimes even helpful, like dusting and cleaning!

Howie may not be the only ghost resident in Government House. There have been reports of the sounds of children laughing and babies crying late at night. Some people also claim to have seen a ghostly face appear beside their own when looking in a mirror in the building. In a building that has been the residence of so many people since its completion in 1891, it should not seem too surprising if it houses more than one ghost. Indeed, who wouldn't want to remain in such a large and beautiful building?

Scary Place Names

Canada
Gore Bay, Ontario
Isle aux Morts, Newfoundland
Mount Lucifer, Alberta
Tombstone Mountain, Yukon

Sorcerer Mountain, British Columbia
Spirit River, Alberta
Spiritwood, Saskatchewan

United States
Bloody Springs, Mississippi
Cape Fear, North Carolina
Coffins Corner, New Jersey
Dark Hollow, Indiana
Deadman Crossing, Ohio
Deadwood, South Dakota
Death Valley, California
Eek, Alaska
Frankenstein, Missouri
Graves Mill, Virginia
Mummy Island, Alaska
Scary, West Virginia
Shivers, Mississippi
Skull Valley, Arizona
Spook City, Colorado
Tombstone, Arizona
Warlock, Texas
Witch Lake, Michigan

Scary Alberta, Canada

 Apparition Mountain and Phantom Crag: This mountain is located in the Banff area. It is reputedly part of an area known for paranormal activity. The crag is nearby.

 Black Cat Mountain: This mountain near Hinton has the appearance of a cat with an arched back.

 Devil's Head Mountain: As the name indicates, this mountain resembles the outline of a face.

Ghost River: This river, located northwest of Calgary, is named for the ghosts said to haunt its banks. According to an old Native legend, a battle took place there. Some time afterwards, a ghost was seen walking along the shore picking up the skulls of the fallen braves.

 Hell-Roaring Creek and Hell-Roaring Falls: Waterton Lakes National Park is home to these two terrifying-sounding places.

 Tombstone Mountain: This mountain, located west of Turner Valley, is named for the numerous slabs of rock seen at its summit.

The Spirit of White Eagle

Many moons ago, according to Stony Legend, the Stony people were at war with the Cree and the Blackfoot. The Stony warriors had just lost a battle to their enemies. Their chief, White Eagle, led them away from the battleground to the mountains in the area of present-day Morley. There, the band regrouped. They were attacked soon afterwards, and White Eagle was seriously injured. Knowing he would die soon, he instructed the braves to carry his body to the top of Devil's Head Mountain and bury him there. After doing so, they were to loosen all the rocks around the grave. The braves did as instructed. The loosened rocks fell down the side of the mountain, killing the Cree and Blackfoot warriors who were coming up to attack the Stony men again.

Victorious in death, the spirit of White Eagle is said to still be seen sometimes, riding his white stallion along the shores of Ghost Lake, down Ghost River and finally back up to the top of Devil's Head. His faithful dog follows close behind.

FAIRS AND FESTIVALS

How About a Haunted Holiday?

Looking to do something a bit different this Halloween? Need the adrenalin rush that a good scare gives you? Several enterprising entrepreneurs have decided to cash in on the burgeoning Halloween market by catering to thrill-seeking tourists. Check out these hot horror spots!

- **Hallowmas Fair**—This is one of the longest running Halloween festivals in the world. It has been an annual event in Edinburgh since at least 1517. The Hallowfair gingerbread sold at the fair is same type sold there four centuries ago.

- **Greenwich Village Parade**—Started in 1973 by the puppeteer and theater director Ralph Lee, this Halloween parade has become the largest of its type in the world. Two million participate in the festivities each year, including a large segment of New York City's gay community. The parade was first broadcast on TV in 2000.

Fantasy Fest—Celebrate this haunted holiday in sunny Key West, Florida, at Fantasy Fest (founded in 1978). These 10 days of entertainment include a parade, costume contests (for both people and pets!), toga parties and celebrity look-alike contests.

Rocky Point—This Halloween theme park is definitely not for the faint of heart. Spread across two locations in Ogden and Salt Lake City, Utah, it is open only for six horrifying weeks before Halloween. Started by Neil Crabtree in 1979, the park includes a number of scary sites, such as the Haunted Museum, Lein Point Cemetery, the Haunted Mansion, the Creepy Classics, Pirates of the Scare-ibbean, Psycho Circus Tent with 3-D clown terrors, Bat Caves, Insane Asylum and the Slasher Wax Museum.

Castle Dracula Hotel—Built in 1983 at the summit of Borgo Pass in the Carpathian Mountains in Transylvania, Romania, this hotel resembles a medieval castle. Guests can visit Dracula's crypt.

Spooky World—This is a family-oriented Halloween theme park located in Foxboro, Massachusetts. David Bertolino and Boneyard Productions created the park in 1991. Among the numerous attractions is the Cirque Macabre in which a young woman lies in a coffin while hundreds of mice and rats scurry over her body. Other venues include the American Horror Museum, the Hayride of Terror, the Catacombs, Creature Feature Haunted Mansion, Professor Nightmare's Experiment, the International Monster Museum, Horrorwood Walk of Fame, Jack-o-lantern Jamboree, Elvira's Nightmare Haunted House, Phantom Mineshaft, 3-D Disco Haunted House, House of Fangs and the Halloween Supermarket.

dEdmonton

The city of Edmonton, Alberta, Canada, has a new and exciting organization dedicated to the promotion of the humor and horror of Halloween. Known as "dEdmonton," and run by a non-profit group, the group's goal is to make this provincial capital also the Halloween capital of the entire country.

Edmonton is already known as the Festival City and is renowned for the fun events that occur in the city and area throughout the year. dEdmonton is hoping to bring together all the Halloween events in the city and area as well as introduce a scary but fun Halloween element.

The board of directors for dEdmonton, affectionately known as the "Council of E-ville," is hoping that the group's efforts will be both a cultural and economic boost for the city. On the organization's website (www.dedmonton.com), visitors and residents alike can find a map of businesses carrying merchandise or offering services for every young and old ghost and ghoul. As well, there is another map showing the locations of various Halloween-related events in the area along with a description of the thrills that await those daring enough to attend!

The Nightmare before Christmas

dEdmonton's entry in the city's Santa Claus parade in 2009 was inspired by Tim Burton's well-known movie, *The Nightmare before Christmas* (1993). Perfect for dEdmonton's goal of bringing a bit of fun-filled fear to every occasion, this movie is about the discovery of Christmas by Jack Skellington, the pumpkin king of Halloween Town. Jack and the other residents of Halloween Town make a failed attempt to take over the other holiday by kidnapping Santa Claus and delivering a bunch of scary toys.

It's Time to Party!

Halloween is synonymous with having a good time—dressing up, fantasizing, scaring people, indulging in sweets, and, for many adults, imbibing. Several distilleries produce alcoholic beverages with a grim twist. Here are some ideas for your next Halloween party!

🍸 England's Wychwood Brewery employs the evil witch motif to sell its **Black Wych Ale**, touted as a "spellbinding stout": *Can you resist the power of the Black Wych?* The label depicts a sexy but naughty witch who stares directly at the viewer.

🍸 Canada's **Crystal Head Vodka** comes in a clear glass bottle shaped like a skull! Its distributors guarantee that it is "pure spirit."

- An English firm produces two types of **Vampyre Vodka**, one of which is blood red in color.

- A Luxembourg firm uses the image of a grinning skull wearing a top hat to promote its **Black Death Vodka**.

- Wine lovers may want to try one of the many wines, such as **True Blood**, **Vampire** and **Dracula**, produced by California's Paso Robles' Vampire Vineyards.

- Two types of Belgian beers feature a picture of a witch dressed in red on the label—**Sublim** and **Promesse**.

- **Captain Morgan's Rum** is named for a swashbuckling Welsh buccaneer who lived during the 17th century. This pirate with his gleaming sword is shown on the label of every variety of rum produced by this company.

- California's Armida Winery produces a wine that is perfect for a frighteningly fun party. **Poizin** comes in a coffin-shaped box. It has a skull-and-crossbones label, and the cork is dipped in blood-red wax. It is advertised as "the wine to die for"!

- Kentucky's Elk Creek Vineyards produces two Halloween wines—**Bone Dry Red** (with a skeleton on the label) and **Ghostly White** (with two handprints on the label).

- Two French wines are named for the mischievous fairies—**Blend of the Fairies** and **Tears of the Fairies**.

DID YOU KNOW?

During the 1870s in the Wild West, whiskey was thought to be a remedy for a tarantula's bite. Thus, whiskey was commonly known as "tarantula juice."

Songs for Your Next Halloween Party

"Abracadabra" by Steve Miller Band (1982)

"All Nightmare Long" by Metallica (2008)

"Bad Moon Rising" by Creedence Clearwater Revival (1969)

"Bat Out of Hell" by Meat Loaf (1977)

"Black Magic Woman" by Santana (1970)

"Black Sabbath" by Black Sabbath (1970)

"Boris the Spider" by The Who (1966)

"Clap for the Wolfman" by Guess Who (1974)

"The Devil Went Down to Georgia" by The Charlie Daniels Band (1979)

"Devil's Den" by Clarence Brewer (1999)

"Disturbia" by Rhianna (2008)

"(Don't Fear) The Reaper" by Blue Oyster Cult (1976)

"Do the Vampire" by Superdrag (1998)

"Fear of the Dark" by Iron Maiden (1992)

"Feed My Frankenstein" by Alice Cooper (1992)

"Flying Dutchman" by McKendree Spring (2007)

"Frankenstein" by Edgar Winter Group (1973)

"Ghostbusters" by Ray Parker Jr. (1984)

"Hells Bells" by AC/DC (1980)

"Highway to Hell" by AC/DC (1979)

"I'm Your Boogieman" by White Zombie (1996)

"I Put a Spell on You" by Screamin' Jay Hawkins (1956)

"I Want Candy" by The Strangeloves (1965)

"Living Dead Girl" by Rob Zombie (1998)

"Monster Is Loose" by Meat Loaf (2006)

"The Monster Mash" by Bobby ("Boris") Pickett (1962)

"Nightmare on My Street" by DJ Jazzy Jeff and the Fresh Prince (1988)

"Psycho Killer" by Talking Heads (1977)

"Purple People Eater" by Sheb Wooley (1958)

"Runnin' with the Devil" by Van Halen (1978)

"Scary Monsters" by David Bowie (1980)

"Season of the Witch" by Donovan (1966)

"Swamp Witch" by Jim Stafford (1973)

"Take the Devil" by The Eagles (1972)

"This House in Haunted" by Alice Cooper (2003)

"Thriller" by Michael Jackson (1982)

"Voodoo Chile" by Jimi Hendrix (1968)

"Welcome to My Nightmare" by Alice Cooper (1975)

"Werewolves of London" by Warren Zevon (1978)

"Wicked Annabella" by The Kinks (1968)

"Wicked Old Witch" by John Fogarty (2004)

"Witch Doctor" by David Seville (1958)

"Witch Queen of New Orleans" by Redbone (1974)

DID YOU KNOW?

Traditionally, "Auld Lang Syne" was sung at the end of Halloween celebrations in Scotland.

WEDDINGS

A Celebration with Style and Spirit(s)

The move today is towards more personalized weddings. Couples are doing all sorts of things to make their weddings unique and to reflect their own individual personalities. One popular trend is the theme wedding. Many of these involve dressing up in costumes, such as medieval-themed weddings. Halloween-themed weddings are also starting to make their mark.

Halloween weddings run the gamut from the more traditional, elegant wedding with Halloween-themed invitations, decorations and favors to the fun, kid-inclusive wedding to the scary, horror wedding. Why do couples choose a Halloween theme for their wedding? Some do so because of an intense love for the holiday. Others are horror movie buffs. Some just want something different.

I Boo!

- Jack Holsinger married Connie Spitznagel at a haunted house attraction near Cleveland, Ohio, in October 2009. The groom arrived at the altar in a coffin, to be married by a minister dressed as Jason of *Friday the 13th* fame. The couple, dressed as vampires, exchanged vows and then the groom bit the bride's neck. The best man was dressed as the pirate Jack Sparrow, while the maid-of-honor was attired in a bride-of-Frankenstein outfit.

- Two mortuary students were married in the Melrose Abbey Mausoleum in Anaheim, California, on Halloween. The groom, in an old-fashioned undertaker's suit, pledged his love for his bride, whose make-up had been done by the cosmetologist of a funeral home.

- Jamie Briggs of New Jersey wore a red-and-black dress to her wedding at the ruins of an old church on Halloween 2009. Following the ceremony, a reception was held with guests donning masks and eating pieces of a wedding cake splattered with fake blood.

- John Leonard and Margaret Gross of Fremont, Ohio, arrived at their wedding, which took place in a haunted house, in caskets.

- Tracy Fox and Nick Adams of Waterbury, Connecticut, chose Halloween 2008 for their wedding because of a mutual love of horror films. The justice of the peace who performed the ceremony dressed as a witch. The ceremony took place in a tattoo parlor.

Following the ceremony, Tracy and Nick each had a word tattooed across their knuckles rather than exchanging rings: Tracy chose "werewolf" while Nick picked "wormfood." A wedding cake shaped like a black cat was then enjoyed by the guests.

NO MORE HALLOWEEN?!

Banning Halloween

Some (mostly fundamentalist) Christians mistakenly believe that Halloween is a celebration of evil. They believe it is a cover for sinister occult practices, like Satan worshipping. Nothing could be further from the truth.

Some people in European countries where Halloween festivities are just being introduced fear that trick-or-treating will only increase the anti-social behavior and vandalism of some youths. While this may occur in cases, those same young people would undoubtedly find another way of accomplishing the same things without Halloween, much as they have for many years.

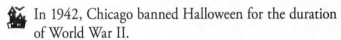 In 1942, Chicago banned Halloween for the duration of World War II.

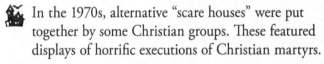 In the 1970s, alternative "scare houses" were put together by some Christian groups. These featured displays of horrific executions of Christian martyrs.

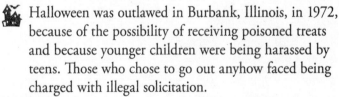 Halloween was outlawed in Burbank, Illinois, in 1972, because of the possibility of receiving poisoned treats and because younger children were being harassed by teens. Those who chose to go out anyhow faced being charged with illegal solicitation.

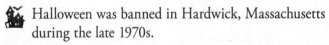 Halloween was banned in Hardwick, Massachusetts during the late 1970s.

In 1986, fundamentalist Ralph Forbes filed a lawsuit against the celebration of Halloween in Arkansas state schools. Forbes denounced the holiday as Devil worshipping. He was unsuccessful in his endeavor.

Since 1997, some American churches have set up alternative haunted houses that focus on "sins" such as abortion and homosexuality.

 In Sandusky, Ohio, it is illegal for anyone over 14 years old to go begging for treats on Halloween.

Is Halloween Too Frightening for You?

Not too fond of things that go bump in the night? The grim decor and costuming of some Halloween events is not for everyone. If you suffer from one of the following phobias, you may prefer to stay indoors hidden under your covers on the night of October 31:

arachnophobia = fear of spiders
cartilogenophobia = fear of bones
chiroptophobia = fear of bats
coimetrophobia = fear of cemeteries
demophobia = fear of demons and evil spirits
hemotophobia = fear of blood
herpetophobia = fear of reptiles and other creepy-crawly things
musophobia = fear of mice and rats
necrophobia = ear of corpses
opidiophobia = fear of snakes
paphophobia = fear of graves
phasmophobia = fear of ghosts
placophobia = fear of tombstones
pneumatiphobia = fear of spirits
sanguivoriphobia = fear of vampires
sciophobia = fear of shadows
teratophobia = fear of monsters
wiccaphobia = fear of witches

Reformation Day

On October 31, 1517, Martin Luther nailed a list of items pertaining to the Catholic Church with which he had an issue. This list became known as *The 95 Theses*. This was the beginning of the Protestant Reformation. Luther eventually established a new church, the Lutheran Church. Today, five states in Germany recognize Lutheranism as their official religion: Brandenburg, Mecklenburg-Vorpommern, Saxony, Saxony-Anhalt and Thuringia. Lutheranism spread around the world with missionaries and colonists.

Lutherans celebrate October 31 as Reformation Day (officially, The Festival of the Reformation). Special church services are held on this day. In the five German states listed above, as well as Slovenia and Chile, the day is a holiday to be spent with family and friends.

THE SPREAD OF HALLOWEEN

Selling Halloween

All across North America in the weeks leading up to Halloween, people can be found decorating their homes and yards in an eerie fashion. Giant cobwebs appear overnight. Ghosts hang from tree branches, swaying in the wind. Scarecrows and grinning pumpkins abound. Front yards suddenly become cemeteries.

These decorations, like costumes, can be costly creations purchased from the growing number of Halloween retailers. They can also be inexpensive projects made by the family throughout the month of October. Either way, they are bound to cause a stir.

In recent years, retailers have been selling more and more decorations alongside the candy and costumes. The holiday has become hugely commercialized and as a result is spreading to other areas of the world, such as Mexico and Europe. However, not everyone in these places is happy with the new holiday, which some say takes away from their more solemn, religious observations for the dead.

Nonetheless, with major international corporations behind the spread, it is unlikely that many countries will be able to halt the trend for long. Interestingly, it is the two European countries of France and Austria that have issued stamps in recognition of Halloween, and not Canada and the U.S., the two main celebrants.

In 2001, France issued a Halloween stamp with a jack-o-lantern on it. In 2004, the country issued another stamp.

This one had a spider descending to a jack-o-lantern. A witch and bats fly in the background.

In 2005, Austria issued a Halloween stamp with a grinning jack-o-lantern in the forefront and an owl, witch and bats in the background.

Canadian Facts and Stats

❀ In 2007, 72 percent of Canadians participated in Halloween festivities.

❀ In 2007, just over half of all Canadians purchased a pumpkin at Halloween.

❀ In 2006, Canadians spent $1.15 billion on Halloween costumes, decorations and treats.

❀ People in British Columbia spend more on Halloween than people in the rest of the country, but those in Alberta spend the most on treats.

❀ People in the Maritimes spend the least amount of money on Halloween.

❀ On average, Canadian men spend more money on Halloween costumes and treats than Canadian women.

❀ In a 2001 survey, 30 percent of Canadians said they believed in ghosts; just over 6 percent claimed to have seen a ghost.

❀ The most popular costumes among Canadian men in 2007 were zombies and pirates.

❀ The most popular costumes among Canadian women in 2007 were pirates, fairies and pumpkin costumes.

❀ The number of pets being dressed in costumes is increasing each year. At present, over 10 percent of pet owners dress their pets up for Halloween.

American Facts and Stats

★ The top five children's costumes in the U.S. in 2009 were princess, witch, Spiderman, pirate and pumpkin/jack-o-lantern.

★ Detroit's Fire Department reported 119 fires on Devil's/Angel's Night (October 30) in 2009.

★ Morton, Illinois, is the self-proclaimed "Pumpkin Capital of the World."

★ In 2008, American farmers produced 1.1 billion pounds of pumpkins.

★ American pet owners who dressed up their dog or cat for Halloween preferred a devil costume above all others.

★ In 2007, one-third of all American adults wore a costume for Halloween.

★ In 2007, Americans spent $5 billion on Halloween costumes, merchandise and treats.

★ Halloween accounts for 25 percent of all candy sold by American manufacturers.

★ Nevada joined the United States on October 31, 1864.

★ In 2008, convicted sex offenders residing in Maryland were required to display signs depicting a jack-o-lantern and stating "No Candy at This Residence."

Miscellaneous Halloween Superstitions

An old American superstition was that wearing earrings on Halloween would result in hearing loss.

An Anglo-Saxon superstition was that if you bled on Halloween, it was a sign that you would die in the near future.

Friends made on Halloween will remain friends for a year (at least). Friends who quarrel on Halloween and fail to make up by midnight will remain at odds for a year.

If you hear someone walking behind you on Halloween, do not look back. It could be Death following you, and it is fatal to look Death in the face.

Baking bread on Halloween night will bring bad luck.

If you see your own shadow by the light of the moon on Halloween, bad luck is sure to follow.

An old English superstition held that if you caught a falling leaf on Halloween, you would have a year filled with happiness.

Stand at a crossroads on Halloween and listen to the wind. It will tell you the most important things that will happen to you in the coming year.

Odds 'n' Ends

Many early 20th-century university students in Canada and the U.S. turned the traditional pranks of Halloween into a freshman hazing ritual. At this time, the school year did not begin until the completion of harvest. The tradition died out when the start of school was pushed back to the beginning of September.

In the early 20th century, Halloween was known as "Thump-the-Door Night" on the Isle of Man because boys would gather outside the home of anyone they did not like and throw turnips and potatoes at the door until the owner gave them money to go away. Occasionally, the boys went too far and complaints or legal action resulted. Eventually, the custom died out.

- Black and orange are the unofficial colors of Halloween. Orange represents the harvest aspects of the festivities, while black is a sign of respect for the dead.

- In Ray Bradbury's 1972 novel, *The Halloween Tree*, an old man guides a group of youths through the history of Halloween.

- In 1974, merchants of Union, New Jersey, were prohibited from selling eggs to anyone under 18, in an attempt to prevent the egging of so many houses on Halloween.

- The half-mile-long Tunnel of Posilipo near Naples, Italy, is completely illuminated by the sun at sunset only on Halloween.

- A special Halloween chili pepper has been bred by New Mexico State University. This miniature pepper, that is too hot to eat, changes from orange to black.

- Halloween is the fifth busiest day of the year for pizza deliveries.

- Over 300 Halloween greeting cards are made by Hallmark.

- The next Halloween to have a full moon will be October 31, 2020.

ABOUT THE ILLUSTRATORS

Peter Tyler

Peter is a recent graduate of the Vancouver Film School Visual Art and Design, and Classical animation programs. Though his ultimate passion is filmmaking, he is also intent on developing his draftsmanship and storytelling, with the aim of using those skills in future filmic misadventures.

Roger Garcia

Roger Garcia is a self-taught artist with some formal training who specializes in cartooning and illustration. He is an immigrant from El Salvador, and during the last few years, his work has been primarily cartoons and editorial illustrations in pen and ink. Recently, he has started painting once more. Focusing on simplifying the human form, he uses a bright, minimal palette and as few elements as possible. His work can be seen in newspapers, magazines and promo material.